jugaad
yatra

jugaad yatra

exploring the indian
art of problem solving

DEAN NELSON

ALEPH

ALEPH

ALEPH BOOK COMPANY
An independent publishing firm
promoted by *Rupa Publications India*

First published in India in 2018
by Aleph Book Company
7/16 Ansari Road, Daryaganj
New Delhi 110 002

ISBN: 978-93-87561-25-0

3 5 7 9 10 8 6 4 2

For sale in the Indian subcontinent only

Printed and bound in India by Parksons Graphics Pvt. Ltd., Mumbai

For Pamela, Charlie, Georgia and Fergus,
for the best yatra of all
and my parents, Reginald and Brenda,
for putting me on the path to them.

CONTENTS

Prologue: A Jugaad Yatra   ix

1. Snowbreeze   1

2. Swadeshi R & D   11

3. Crorepatis: The Jugaad Guide to Making Billions   29

4. 'For Most Indians 70 Per Cent Is Good Enough'   49

5. Bad Jugaad   65

6. A River Runs Through It   90

7. The Grand Trunk Road to Nowhere   105

8. Urban Jugaad: India's Cities in Crisis   118

9. Yatra's End: A T-Point on Jugaad Marg   145

Acknowledgements   157

Notes and References   159

A JUGAAD YATRA

Jugaad

Joo-gaard (retroflex r)

Hindi feminine noun. Colloquial mean. a quick fix, improvised or home-made solution, a frugal innovation, a temporary hack, botch job, bypass, by any means necessary, corruption. Provision, means of providing. To gather together the necessary means to do something.

2014: A Space Oddity

Wednesday, 24 September 2014, was, arguably, one of the greatest days in India's long and rich history. Scientists at the Indian Space Research Organisation (ISRO) had fired a rocket to Mars and put their *Mangalyaan* spacecraft into its orbit.

The seventh-largest economy in the world and projected to be the fifth largest (overtaking Britain and France by the end of 2018), India was finally coming into its own. For too many years its image had been stereotyped by poverty, its popular Bollywood song and dance films and Mahatma Gandhi, the patron saint of non-violent protest and father of modern, independent India. Now, suddenly, *Mangalyaan's* success compelled the world to look afresh at India. It was not only an interplanetary pioneer, one of only four nations to have completed a mission to Mars, it was the only one to succeed at its first attempt. It was a moment of bursting national pride and there were scenes of jubilation at ISRO's mission control where

Prime Minister Narendra Modi joined its scientists to celebrate their extraordinary success and the manner in which they had achieved it.

Its great achievement, however, wasn't to boldly go where no mission had gone before but to establish itself as the undisputed leader in shoestring space travel. It had cost just $74 million, almost one-tenth of the $671 million spent by the rival American *MAVEN* mission, and less than the production budget of *Gravity*, the Oscar-winning Hollywood space thriller starring George Clooney and Sandra Bullock, the Indian prime minister had noted. How did India do that? The secret of India's Mars Orbiter Mission (MOM), according to its scientists, was in its reliance on 'jugaad'—a wide-ranging term that refers to inspiring, frugal inventions, ingenious innovations which defy conventional wisdom; but also to corruption, a ruse to beat the system and to flout or bypass the rules.

The word is also used to refer to hybrid trikes popular on Indian roads: the wheel, steering column and frame of an old Enfield Bullet motorbike welded to a home-made chassis attached to a carriage or trailer, often powered by a water pump motor. The variations are infinite but all assembled from assorted scrap powered by something intended for a different purpose altogether. This original jugaad was made possible when the late Prime Minister Indira Gandhi distributed cheap pumps to poor farmers to boost food production. But on holidays they were used as engines to power a new kind of vehicle to ferry worshippers to temples and families to weddings.

In India, the word isn't just a simple noun but a popular adjective too: a jugaad solution is usually rough, quick and improvised, relying on immediately available, discarded or broken materials no longer good for their original use. A leaking car radiator repaired by a roadside mechanic with bubble gum, a coat-hanger radio aerial, canvas tarpaulins which billow up to double the loads of top-heavy haulage trucks, the adapted rear wheel stands and chains which turn boneshaker bicycles into knife sharpeners.

And from noun and adjective, it has risen to verb status. To do some jugaad is to find a way around a problem by any means necessary, from inspired improvisation to the payment of a bribe. A candidate who has just failed his driving test might plead with his examiner: 'Bhai saab, kuch jugaad kar do?' (Sir, please, do some jugaad for me?) A thousand rupees might be what it costs to pass without taking the test or for the examiner to find another way of looking at it. It might be the factory owner's resort when the government inspector notices he is pumping illegal chemical waste effluents into a river. It might be the inspector's solution to make it a monthly payment.

Jugaad, then, describes funny, inspiring, frugal inventions, instant innovations, but can also refer to corruption, bending the rules and beating the system. In all its uses there is an element of circumvention, of 'bypassing' a problem. It can be good, bad, helpful or dangerous. So what part could this rough and ready approach have played in the most advanced, demanding rocket science of India's triumphant mission to Mars? The scientists at ISRO had turned to jugaad when they attempted what appeared to be Mission Impossible: to fire a spacecraft to Mars on a rocket which did not have the conventional power to get there and to build it in three years using local materials and personnel for less than the cost of a studio-based space movie. Their American counterparts at NASA would, almost certainly, have shaken their heads and said it just could not be done without a bigger, better and costlier rocket. Our Indian heroes, however, simply got to work and made do with the materials they had.

Instead of creating a purpose-built rocket powerful enough to reach the red planet, they dusted down their own Polar Satellite Launch Vehicle (PSLV), designed more than twenty years earlier to put small satellites in orbit above the Earth. To keep costs low, they ditched NASA's iterative model where each component and stage is tested before the next begins, and built a rocket using cobbled together parts from earlier models, all in one go. What they could not do, for all their ingenuity, was supercharge a rocket made to launch Earth satellites into one that could carry its payload all the way to Mars. Conventional thinking was a black hole.

Their solution was to think of a way to bypass the problem they couldn't crack to one they could. So instead of pointing their patchwork rocket at Mars, they first had it loop the Earth for a month to build momentum. By keeping it in an increasing elliptical orbit and firing its burners intermittently, the scientists simply worked around its obvious shortcomings, overcame its power deficit and set their rocket on a circuitous flight to glory. They had launched *Mangalyaan* in much the same way David slew Goliath—a cosmic slingshot method. They had cut corners, made do with recycled parts, rejected conventional wisdom and flown by the seat of their pants.

It could so easily have failed. The burners had not initially succeeded in raising the rocket's orbit to the correct height and extra blasts were ordered in those anxious moments when the mission hovered between success and failure. ISRO's scientists held their nerve and at the eleventh hour, the burners finally lifted the rocket to the required trajectory, stone shot from sling and the rest is space history.

Alok Chatterjee, a former ISRO scientist working with NASA who liaised between the two space agencies, paid tribute to the part jugaad had played in the mission's success and defined it as the 'Indian approach of getting the maximum out of spending the least amount of resources, including time.'

'And while jugaad cannot defy the laws of physics in getting a complex space mission like MOM accomplished, it is definitely a time-tested approach that has proved applicable to processes for achieving the mission's accelerated goals,' he told the American management consultant Karine Schomer.

It was a higher tech, interplanetary equivalent of a home-made jugaad trike winning the Monaco Grand Prix and in victory *Mangalyaan* had not only waved the nation's tricolour across the heavens, it had fired a very Indian way of thinking into outer space.

It gave a huge boost to national confidence and made possible another giant step just over two years later, in February 2017, when ISRO launched 104 satellites from a single rocket to set a new world record.

Mangalyaan's mission to Mars was India's 'Man on the Moon' moment, a source of deep pride and joy for a nation that has suffered more than its fair share of hardship. So it was all the more intriguing that at its moment of greatest triumph observers chose to celebrate the role jugaad thinking had played in it. Not least because Indians themselves are fiercely divided on whether jugaad is a source of pride or shame—a competitive advantage and entrepreneurial force behind the country's rise or a byword for cheap, shoddy products, a cause of chaos and enduring underachievement. The dispute touches on essential questions of how Indians see themselves, their skills, traits and achievements as a nation, their hopes, aspirations and potential as also—how they want the world to think about their country.

◆

Throughout 2015 and 2016, the Twitter hashtag, #JugaadNation became a social media sensation with popular websites like BuzzFeed showcasing the 'hilariously creative ways Indians get shit done no matter what'. There was a bicycle where a missing handlebar was replaced with a car steering wheel, a broken shower head replaced with a taped plastic water bottle pricked with dozens of holes at the bottom. Household irons were shown being used to straighten women's curls or upturned as hotplates to boil milk. Air conditioner units with missing grills became chillers for beer while a desert cooler was adapted to cool two neighbouring rooms by attaching a pair of old trousers to divide the flow, one leg for each. There were pressure cookers propped up by two bottles and heated by burning candles taped together, a shattered clock missing numbers 1 to 7 made good with the digits scrawled onto the wall on which it hung, and endless varieties of crop-sprayers and ploughs made from bicycle wheels, discarded oil barrels and bits of old scrap metal.

There were stories too, along with pictures. In November 2016, when Narendra Modi scrapped ₹1,000 and ₹500 banknotes to target black money and corruption, India's ATM machines were suddenly under siege and customers were forced to queue for many hours to get cash. Satjeet Singh Bedi had a jugaad solution to hand—he set up BookMyChotu.com to supply labourers to stand in line on behalf of the well-to-do who could hire a chotu—which literally means 'little one'—for ₹90 per hour to take the pain out of Modi's demonetization.

These pictures and tales went viral on a global wave of LOLs and OMGs, shared by Indians as a celebration of their inspiring resourcefulness and optimism amid scarcity and poverty. It reflected the extent to which jugaad had been claimed as a treasured 'we are like that, only' Indian trait.

In his book, *India's Century: The Age of Entrepreneurship in the World's Biggest Democracy*, veteran Congress leader and former cabinet minister Kamal Nath described how jugaad creativity had blossomed in the hardship of India's early post-independence years. The shortage economy—when Jawaharlal Nehru's government curbed imports and restricted foreign investment in favour of domestic production—demanded frugality and turned 'every Indian' into a 'master of jugaad'.

The word describes 'as nothing else does the ability to creatively "manage", to make do with quick fix solutions. Jugaad developed into a survival skill for most Indians. It was the additional resource that gave greater returns within a framework of scarcity. Every obstacle thus became an opportunity, a showcase for ingenuity... I sometimes wonder whether jugaad, a form of scientific innovation, represents a suppressed Indian inventive gene,' he wrote.

In recent years, the idea of jugaad itself has been repackaged as an Indian export, a business philosophy with answers for lumbering Western companies desperate to transform their fortunes in a time of austerity. If only they could embrace India's flexibility and frugal innovation they too could strip out costs and achieve 'breakthrough growth', its proponents claim.

There is no shortage of studies to support their case. Tata, India's revered BPO-to-steel conglomerate, created the Nano, the world's cheapest car, by making its record low price—₹1 lakh—the starting point of its design. The same frugal approach developed a stripped-down ₹1,200 water purifier. Well-known cardiac surgeon Dr Devi Shetty has cut the cost of coronary bypass operations to less than ₹1.3 lakh at his no-frills Narayana Health 'factory' hospitals—one-sixth of the cost in Britain and an even tinier fraction of the bill at the United States' celebrated Cleveland Clinic. His surgeons conduct up to thirty-five operations a day compared to the two an American counterpart might do. He believes he will soon be able to do them for around ₹50,000 while poor patients are treated free of charge. The inventors of the Aakash used only the most basic components and rethought what was truly necessary to produce the world's cheapest tablet computer for a little more than ₹2,000, an iPad for the poor.

Jugaad innovation isn't reserved for inventions, it is about processes too, a way of thinking. Indians have, for example, pioneered the language of the 'missed call'—a basic code based on the number of rings—as a free communication system. One ring might mean I'm on my way, two please call me back, three might be something serious. No one picks up, and no one's credit balance is debited.

The examples are endless and for its supporters they are evidence of a 'Jugaad Nation' on the move and an inspiration for the world to fall in line. Some parts of the world have taken the advice to heart. A British government-funded report by the innovation think tank, Nesta, suggested that jugaad could be 'a route to innovation success in the UK' and 'a strategic focus for collaboration' between India and the United Kingdom. 'A culture of "jugaad", or creative improvisation, means the unusual skill set and mindset required for frugal innovation are abundant,' the report argued and quoted its leading gurus' definition: 'First, it is frugal: it enables innovators to get more with less. Second, it is flexible: it enables innovators to keep experimenting and rapidly change course when needed. Third, it is democratic: it can therefore tap into the wisdom of otherwise marginalized customers and employees.'

But while jugaad may be 'practised by almost all Indians in their daily lives to make the most of what they have', its critics are equally convinced that it's a daunting obstacle in the path of India's social and economic development. For them jugaad is a byword for cute but shoddy products, ad hoc decision-making, poor compliance, weak systems, organizational chaos and disregard for standards or excellence. For those who want to see India competing with and leading the world, jugaad is one of the reasons why it often falls short. They see India's love of the quick fix in the weakness of its research and development and failure to build respected, enduring systems. The jugaad trike might be a quirky icon of frugal ingenuity but it is also a symbol of backwardness, poor governance and a mark of India's failure to move beyond 'make do and mend' to pioneering technology.

If politics is the art of the possible, jugaad thinking has certainly broadened the horizons of India's politicians. Anger over the growth in graft was widely acknowledged to have been a key factor in the 'Modi wave' which swept his Bharatiya Janata Party (BJP) to landslide victories in the 2014 general election and the Uttar Pradesh state assembly elections in 2017. An insight into the scale of corruption under the Congress government he ousted emerged in 2011 when secret American diplomatic cables were published by WikiLeaks. One US diplomat reported being shown two chests containing cash by a political aide as the party fought to survive a parliamentary confidence vote in 2008. The money was to bribe Members of Parliament (MPs) to support the government after its Communist coalition partners withdrew support in protest over a civil nuclear energy agreement with the United States. Senior political leader Amar Singh was arrested for offering to bribe BJP MPs but later discharged by the court. He described the confidence vote as India's 'biggest jugaad' in which MPs jailed for murder and extortion had been released to vote and the national interest was traded for party or personal advantage.

Jugaad quick fix solutions and circumvention are, it seems, at the heart of India's greatest triumphs and moments of shame. How can the same word be used so readily to describe a country's successes and its failures?

Bharatbala Ganapathy, popularly known by his first name, was faced with exactly this dilemma when he was asked to direct the opening ceremony for the 2010 Commonwealth Games held in Delhi. The Games were intended to be a soft relaunch for India, a moment to show the world it was no longer a Third World nation but 'Incredible India', all set to leapfrog China as the world's fastest-growing major economy. A Metro system was built in record time, a new airport terminal opened on schedule, but with just days to go before the opening ceremony, these snapshots of the new India gave way to familiar images of the old—chaos and corruption, shoddy workmanship and squalor.

Unfinished roofs yielded to monsoon rains, a footbridge collapsed and athletes arrived to find stray dogs defecating in their apartments. Some national teams threatened to pull out while one local official dismissed their concerns as cultural differences—some nations had different standards of hygiene, he explained. An enquiry by the Comptroller and Auditor General (CAG) later found some of the mismanagement had in fact been deliberate—essential works had been delayed so that the organizers could override procurement rules and give lucrative contracts to favoured bidders. The head of the organizing committee, a senior Congress leader, was later arrested on corruption charges. What was supposed to be a celebration of India's arrival as an international power was suddenly a global public relations disaster but it was Bharatbala's job to put on a great opening show regardless.

His challenge was to make his fellow 1.2 billion Indians feel proud of who they are and what their civilization had achieved amid all the chaos and corruption they see around them in their daily lives; to show the world the best of India when it had just seen so much of its worst.

Rather than gloss over it, he choreographed the chaos against a 5,000-year tableau of Indian culture and civilization in a joyous celebration of everything Indians were proud of and all the problems they could only laugh about. Hundreds of turbaned drummers beat out the rhythms as classical dance troupes clad in every colour moved to different tempos, all at once.

The model of an Indian Railways locomotive steamed into the arena at the head of a carnival procession from India's streets and bazaars. Sergeant Pepper wedding bands marched behind big-headed civil service babus and white Ambassador cars—old Morris Oxfords, salvaged and reinvented as the carriage of high-handed officialdom. Delivery boys wobbled by on boneshaker bicycles, dodging rickshaws piled high with oversized melons, while coolies carrying tall headloads of bricks staggered, zigzag, through the melee. The show perfectly captured the mixed feelings of the moment: deep pride in one of the world's oldest cultures, exasperation with bent officials and politicians and unbridled joy in its chaos and energy.

Jugaad, he explained later, had been his unspoken theme. 'Today's India is chaotic, I would say, noise not music, but in this noise there is a sense of convergent living... Look at our festivals—Holi—it's chaotic and civil, energy and passion. It's our way of life,' he said.

That the same word, jugaad, could be used to describe two completely contrasting events—the triumphant orbiting of Mars and the chaos, waste and corruption of Delhi's Commonwealth Games—fascinated me.

For Bharatbala there was no mystery in it. 'It's like karma—[there's] good jugaad and bad jugaad' and the best kind is frugal, he explained. 'Jugaad is an understanding of identity in empowerment, a common man's self-confidence because he can find a way to make things happen,' he said.

It is one of the means by which Indians survive and prosper in the midst of 'epic chaos' and there is 'order and beauty' in it, he added.

◆

Where does this jugaad—good and bad—come from? How did it weave itself into Bharatbala's national narrative and become not only a means of survival in chaos but the secret of India's global business success and cosmic conquest?

There isn't a single, compelling answer but there are numerous hints and clues. Many of them are from India's ancient scriptures and spiritual epics and the best of them focuses on the story of Lord Ganesha, the universally loved, elephant-headed remover of obstacles and God of new beginnings.

His story, one of many of how Lord Ganesha came by his elephant head, is a 'famous buddhi' or wisdom told to Indian children to teach flexibility and creativity. Swami Nikhilananda of the Chinmaya Mission told me: Parvati had created him from her own skin to keep her company while her consort, Lord Shiva, was away. When he returned Shiva mistook Ganesha for an intruder and beheaded him. When he saw Parvati's grief, he vowed to bring him back to life. 'He sent his man and told him any animal, any person you find, you cut the head of that person and you bring [it to me]. So they went in search and found an elephant, cut the head of the elephant and it was attached to his [Ganesha's] body. I find this as a very good example of jugaad only,' he explained.

The origins of frugal jugaad thinking are also to be found in Lord Krishna's revelation in the Bhagavad Gita that he lives in every object and being, said Swami Nikhilananda. Divinity is in every broken cup, discarded tyre and rusted chassis—they retain their value and potential.

'Still they can serve us. You are using a pen, that pen is serving a purpose, it is inbuilt in me that I should revere it. And just because it is a little loose here and there, I do not throw it out, I'll repair it and continue using it. Of course in these times we are changing it, but it is there in our culture,' he said, 'everyone is jugaading.'

Some believe India's ancient scriptures and texts may also hold the secrets of jugaad's darker side—the corner-cutting, circumvention of ethics, rules and laws, bribery and corruption which often overshadow the best of India.

One particular passage from the Mahabharata, which tells the story of the epic battle for power between two sides of a royal family and the eternal fight all of us face to do the right thing, is often cited as a key reference. Attaining its present form around 400 CE, the epic focuses on the rift between the avaricious Kauravas whose crown prince Duryodhana cheats his righteous Pandava cousins, led by 'dharma prince' Yudhisthira, of their inheritance. When the two sides finally clash at Kurukshetra, the Pandavas find they are no match for the Kaurava general, Drona, whose battlefield prowess threatens to swiftly annihilate them. Lord Krishna urges Yudhisthira to 'stop his fighting by any means possible'—to fool him into believing his son Aswathama has been killed and strike him as he reels in shock. An elephant, which shared his son's name is then slain and when rumours reached Drona that 'Aswathama' is dead, he asks Yudhisthira, known to have never uttered a lie, if it is true.

'Yes it is true,' Yudhisthira replies, but adds, in a whisper: 'an elephant called Aswathama!' Drona is beheaded as he slumps in grief. Yudhisthira, the righteous 'dharma prince', wins the war but goes to hell for a short period for his deceit, while his defeated Kaurava cousin rises to heaven.

Author Amish Tripathi, whose Shiva Trilogy novels have sold more than 2.5 million copies, was nine when he first heard the epic. He couldn't understand why the good guys were plunged into hell. His parents explained that Indian epics are meant to provoke deep questions rather than offer simple answers.

'Through the questions that emerge you will find answers. And you will find philosophies that will make sense to you...your answers can be different from my answers, that's also okay because you're different from me,' Tripathi explained.

This absence of prescriptive answers has spawned 'a self-reliant, creative, independent culture' in which people solve their own problems rather than wait for gods, rulers or others to offer one.

The problem, he conceded, is moral relativism, where right and wrong are matters of personal conscience and interest.

As the writer Gurcharan Das said in his study of the Mahabharata, *The Difficulty of Being Good*, if God is not the final arbiter of good behaviour, where does that leave the individual? They are left alone to 'decide how best to order their lives. Given the plurality of authorities, one has to rely on oneself.'

Some have suggested that clues to the roots of bad jugaad governance could be traced to the *Arthashastra*, the ancient treatise on statecraft by Chanakya who guided Chandragupta Maurya to create an empire which stretched from Bengal in the east to Afghanistan in the west. The text, written around 2,000 years ago, is concerned with perpetuating the rule of the king and warding off threats to his power via different means. Among other things, it describes in detail the ways in which civil servants may cheat the public and how the king may fleece his people when his coffers are low. Its suggestions include the deployment of prostitutes and spies to steal money from businessmen to the building of fake temples to divert donations into the treasury.

Some believe India's caste divisions have helped create the context in which rough jugaad solutions thrived while its early advantage in scientific discovery was squandered. The roads plied by homemade junkyard trikes today were once walked upon by global pioneers of science. Aryabhata named the first ten decimal places, the basis of our modern digital revolution, employed the value of pi and grasped vital aspects of the solar system around 1,500 years ago. Sushruta carried out surgeries like rhinoplasty and lithotomy in around 600 BCE, while the Indus Valley Civilization gave the world advanced urban planning and public sanitation at Mohenjo-Daro, Sindh, more than 4,000 years ago. The celebrated Bengali chemist, Sir Prafulla Chandra Ray, believed the march of Indian science was hobbled by restrictions on what practical actions high-caste Brahmins could do and their relationships with lower-caste artisans and craftsmen who could build on their ideas. Dissecting human cadavers, for example, was an essential element of medical progress, but Brahmins were forbidden from wielding the lancet. Anatomy and surgery became 'lost sciences' while India's artisans were 'left very much to themselves and guided solely by their mother wit and sound common sense,' he wrote.

His argument begs the question: Without these divisions could India's space programme have ticked off Mars long before its American rivals? Would its scientists and innovators now be leading the world? In her essay on jugaad thinking in India's Mars mission, management consultant Karine Schomer suggested caste was only one possible factor and that Mughal invasion and British colonial rule had been significant causes too. A legacy of uncertainty caused by conquest and arbitrary government had created a jugaad 'habit of mind' which 'emphasizes ad hoc improvisation and flexibility as a way of getting things done...without necessarily being concerned about long-term sustainability or systemic impacts,' she wrote. 'Under feudalism, colonialism and—later on—the "bureaucracy Raj" of the first forty years of independent India, the ability to work around the system, to improvise and to circumvent the rules, was often required for any kind of success,' she explained.

Bestselling author and politician Shashi Tharoor has argued in his book, *An Era of Darkness*, that India was in fact leading the world until its economy was sabotaged by British colonial rule. Its handloom weavers made the world's finest muslins until the British 'smashed their thumbs, broke their looms, imposed tariffs and duties on their cloth and products and started taking the raw materials from India and shipping back manufactured cloth,' he wrote. He further pointed out in the book that India's share of world trade slumped from 23 per cent at the beginning of the raj to below 4 per cent at independence in 1947.

The political freedom India later discovered was bound by an extreme poverty compounded by Partition—millions of refugees from East and West Pakistan who lost everything in the exodus and had to rebuild their lives from scratch, broken supply chains, truncated roads and rail tracks.

The conditions required frugality and rewarded affordable innovation. Whatever its origins, India's social, legal, scientific and political landscape is strewn with good and bad, heartening and self-defeating examples of jugaad thinking. It may not be in India's DNA, as some believe, but it has got under its skin—it is a recognizably Indian phenomenon and an underappreciated factor in some of the best and worst aspects of Indian life. This book is a 'jugaad yatra' to explore a distinctly Indian art of problem solving and its impact, good and bad, on modern India.

CHAPTER 1

SNOWBREEZE

Mr M. B. Lal could be forgiven a little swagger—he had just invented a potentially revolutionary air conditioner which promised to make a comfort essential of India's rich affordable to millions of its sweating poor. But it's not his way and in any case his swagger days are long behind him. Now eighty-eight years old, he can just about walk with the aid of a stick. His cheeks are whiskery and hollowed, his clothes baggy on his bent, skeletal frame and his eyes are magnified to saucer size by thick bottle glass spectacles. He is so frail he can meet visitors only in a brief and shifting afternoon slot.

He's not motivated by money or interested in status or glory. What he wants is to share his discovery and make life a little more tolerable for the wretched masses melting in the furnace temperatures of the Indian summer.

What I wanted was a good story for my newspaper and a solution to a looming domestic crisis. We had just moved house in Delhi as part of an austerity drive—away from our once lavish but now dysfunctional suburban farmhouse, with its empty, mould-encrusted pool and balding tennis court, to an old, down-at-heel semi-detached house in Delhi's whiffy Nizamuddin West colony, close to the capital's sewage nullah.

Our youngest son, then eleven, had drawn the short straw—'like always' he complained—and been lumbered with the worst bedroom. It was landlocked between his older sister's and brother's brighter, airier rooms, had no window to the outside world and no exterior wall through which an air conditioner could be fixed to cool it. Come the summer it would be more tandoor than a place to chill. Without a solution to the rising room temperature, there would be frayed tempers, accusations of favouritism and irresistible demands to move yet again to a more functional—and expensive—home.

I'd thought about one of the new ceiling-mounted air conditioners then starting to appear in some of the city's fancier restaurants, but ruled it out for the same reasons which had brought us to the sewer-side neighbourhood in the first place. I needed something to cool the room without burning a hole in my pocket. I needed a quick fix jugaad solution.

And then one February morning, as I hacked my way through *The Hindu*'s newsprint jungle of caste murders, female foeticides and corruption scandals, Mr Lal's Snowbreeze wafted out of its pages like a breath of fresh air. A retired journalist from Kolkata's venerable *The Statesman* newspaper, it reported, had invented a low-cost, ice-based cooling machine which barely consumed the electricity of a humble household light bulb. It reduced indoor temperatures by as much as 7 °C in an hour. But while branded air conditioners start at around ₹16,000 and cost several thousand rupees a month to run in Delhi's long, searing summers, the Snowbreeze could be built by your local electrician and carpenter for less than ₹5,000.

Under the headline 'Beating the heat with a home-made AC', the paper described the Snowbreeze as a 'movable device' which can be 'assembled from scratch at home, with the following easily available components—a container bucket, a few strips of plywood, an ice drum, a roll of aluminium foil and, obviously, loads of ice.

'At the heart of the machine resides a powerful 23-watt fan that propels cool air while wheels at the base ensure that the device can be moved around without too much trouble,' the reporter explained.

Its inventor, Mr Lal, suggested his Snowbreeze could be an answer to India's energy crisis. 'Power shortages, outages and the resulting pollution are being widely discussed these days. This new invention has the potential of cutting down energy consumption by air conditioning and room heating by at least half. It also ensures uninterrupted service during power breakdowns,' he said.

His machine was an 'open source' solution which could be 'rigged up by two carpenters within two days,' he added. Two days worked for me and if his Snowbreeze was anywhere near as effective as the breathless article in *The Hindu* suggested, we would not only be able to stay in our cheap house, but also save money on electricity bills.

I found his booklet online—'Make Your Own Air-Conditioner-Cum-Heater'—and gazed at the cover photograph. The Snowbreeze looked like a *Doctor Who* villain, a home-made dalek costume for a children's fancy-dress party. Its square fan looked like a loudhailer face, it had handles for arms and moved on wheels. It didn't look like the sleek, remote-controlled, Korean-made air conditioners cooling our other rooms and it crossed my mind that its home-made ugliness might embarrass our youngest when his friends came to visit. But it was too late. *The Hindu* had me at Snowbreeze and the idea of an octogenarian offering low-cost cooling for India's rural poor was a tale worth chasing.

By early March it was getting steadily hotter every day so there was no time to lose. I bounded into my stuttering but stately Ambassador car and headed out to the city's Press Enclave, a haven of 1960s concrete apartments set in lush gardens and overlooked by some of the smart new glass and steel shopping malls slowly encircling and modernizing the capital.

I found Mr Lal sitting on a home-made office seat—a cushioned dining chair mounted on castors—working at a small desk with tiny wheels attached to its legs, each adapted to overcome his immobility. He rose slowly to his feet and pointed his walking stick at the solution to my looming summer crisis: a blue plastic dustbin resting on a square skateboard with a boxy fan protruding from its lid and a plastic tap at its base. It is, he explained, a tube of wooden hoops covered in low-grade sheet metal, each notched at a different point on the circumference to slowly suck the air around two ice-filled, stainless-steel tins and blow it out cool.

The idea had come to him as he sat dripping in 35 °C heat during one of the city's regular summer power cuts. He couldn't afford a diesel generator to keep his air conditioners working through the 'outage'. They consumed too much electricity to be fuelled by the battery-based 'inverters' used widely in India to keep lights and fans working when the power fails. So he did what generations of Indians have had to do—he began searching for his own jugaad solution.

As a teenage schoolboy he had run away from home and headed for Mahatma Gandhi's Sevagram Ashram in Maharashtra where he'd hoped to join his freedom movement, but was sent back and told he'd be more help later when he'd finished his studies. In the sweltering train carriages he saw hot and bothered colonial officials being cooled by fans whirring over big blocks of ice on steel trays.

The memory was his Eureka moment. He called in his local electrician and a carpenter—and began to develop the Snowbreeze. 'I first borrowed a tin from my wife in which we keep flour. I put ice in it, put the tin in a wooden box and blew air, then slowed down the air, made it cooler and cooler and then I kept on and on and on, I tried all kinds of tricks,' he explained.

He'd drawn on his own family history of innovation too. In 1840, his great-grandfather had been a supervisor on an East India Company project to build a canal and dam near their home in Saharanpur district, near Haridwar, the Hindu pilgrimage city on the banks of the Ganga in what was then the United Provinces—now known as Uttar Pradesh. One of his tasks had been to follow a senior Company official around the local villages, carrying a covered head-load basket filled with rupee coins to pay the bribes needed to speed up the canal project. Later, during the 1857 Uprising, his great-grandfather saved the official's life and was rewarded with a zamindari.

His family became the wealthiest in the district and some of Mr Lal's earliest memories are of his nana or maternal grandfather making things. He had been a tinkerer who built donkey carts and later made their home the first in the area to have electric lights.

He'd read a newspaper advertisement on the benefits of electrification and immediately bought large batteries to light up his home. 'In the villages there was no electricity; he ordered the batteries, fitted them in his two-storey haveli and got electricity, just for show. They had a special tutor, an MA in history from Agra, and in that classroom and adjoining room he put bulbs, so he was a bit inventive and kept that tradition all along,' he said. However, his own family's yearning for modernity and progress was not shared in his district where even the wealthy slept on charpoys and shunned dining tables. Furniture was considered a Muslim or British affectation and invention a colonial eccentricity, he said.

When he later studied at Allahabad's Ewing Christian College, he noticed how the American missionary teachers were constantly making and repairing things. His own teacher had made himself a chair, a bespoke cushioned couch for his two dogs, while in the workshop farming implements—hoes, pushcarts, lawnmowers—were fabricated and repaired. To his young mind, invention was something that 'came from the West'.

He had noticed an upsurge in jugaad improvisation shortly after India's independence in 1947 when new import controls aimed at protecting its domestic markets suddenly put many Western goods beyond reach. The combination of scarcity—the supply of spare parts for many imported goods was also stopped—and the influx of millions of Sikh and Hindu refugees who fled Pakistan after Partition sparked a surge of creativity and invention, he explained. 'There was this exodus of refugees from Punjab, they started all kinds of things in the early fifties, bicycles, motor dynamos, motor parts, kitchen mixies, anything which was made abroad and whose import was banned, these Punjabis did jugaad on everything and made everything,' he said. Many of them—more than seven million—had left homes and businesses behind them in what became Pakistan and arrived in India with little more than the clothes they wore, a few pieces of hidden jewellery and the trauma of having seen close family and friends murdered in communal violence.

Small mechanical workshops sprang up as those dispossessed sought to rebuild and start anew. The Munjal brothers, who later founded one of India's most successful companies, had blazed the same trail three years before Partition. They began manufacturing bicycle parts before setting up their Hero bicycle workshop in Ludhiana in 1956. Today it is the world's largest two-wheeler manufacturer and an enduring symbol of India's common man. Mr Lal is different, a writer and intellectual, but also a proud jugaadi who shares the same heritage as the Munjal brothers and the millions of other Indians who seek home-made ahead of off-the-shelf solutions.

As his wife puts two tiny china cups of chai and a plate of biscuits on his wheelie table, he explained his excitement at his discovery of ice-based cooling and its revolutionary potential for India and other poor countries where power is scarce. I was smitten. Only weeks before we had been forced to move by the greed of our multi-millionaire landlady who had omitted to tell us our farmhouse flooded every monsoon—all of our clothes and furniture were ruined in the first rain. There was an outstanding electricity bill of more than ₹3 lakh from before our arrival which she did not intend to pay. BSES (Bombay Suburban Electric Supply) officials said not only was the account in arrears, but the landlady had fraudulently claimed a subsidized tariff for poor farmers. Our electricity supply would be disconnected within days if the bill was not settled immediately. When challenged, the landlady said she wouldn't pay but not to worry because we could use a chugging diesel tractor engine to power our home instead.

We moved out a few days later, disillusioned, warier and increasingly sceptical. So when I heard Mr Lal's enthusiasm and saw his earnest desire to make something to help the poor, I wasn't just smitten, I felt tearful. It was hard to believe possible in a man of his years, experience and frailty. He had lived through colonial occupation, seen the misery of Partition and the scarcity and hardship it brought. He had witnessed the brutality of Indira Gandhi's Emergency and India's plunge into institutional corruption in the years following it. And yet he had retained his optimism: his Snowbreeze was just like him—it inhaled cynicism and blew out cool, refreshing wafts of hope. I wanted a piece of it and put a deposit down there and then. For ₹6,000, he, his carpenter and Naveen, the electrician, would build me a Snowbreeze in less than a week and salvage our family's India adventure.

When the Snowbreeze arrived at our home a week or so later, I decided not to allow its strange appearance to nurture doubt. It was a large blue plastic dustbin with a raised lid mounted on a square, aquamarine skateboard. Our house was already well-off for weird—we had a purdah room, an internal courtyard, a manhole drain in the dining room and now we had a Snowbreeze too.

My wife rolled her eyes, our youngest son was indulgent—another one of Dad's mad schemes—and our eldest two, then thirteen and fifteen, just laughed.

As the late afternoon sun sank over the colony and Humayun's Tomb beyond, I couldn't wait to power it up. Our freezer could not possibly produce 20 kilograms of ice, so I called the burfwala from nearby Bhogal market. A delivery boy was dispatched by bicycle with a large block of melting ice wrapped in a dirty, wet rag attached by an elastic bungee strap to the rear wheel rack. By the time he arrived, the 20-kilogram block had melted by a quarter and stood in a puddle of its former self. The burfwala lifted what remained onto the floor, took a mallet and chisel and smashed it into tiny pieces. He scooped up the chunks with his hands and put them into two stainless steel milk containers which were taken upstairs to our son's room and inserted into the Snowbreeze. Our courtyard garden below was now a periglacial lake and I switched on Mr Lal's machine hoping it would have the same cooling effect on the room.

According to Mr Lal's calculations, the summer sun would heat the room to a maximum night temperature of 35 °C, and the Snowbreeze would bring it back down by 7 °C to 28 °C—10 degrees above the lowest setting on the branded air conditioners in the other rooms, but reasonably comfortable.

We closed the door and checked every hour or so to see if it was living up to its promise.

It seemed to be working but I couldn't wait for our son to wake the following morning to hear his verdict. 'It's fine, it works,' he said, and that was good enough for me.

All technology changes the way we live but the Snowbreeze had a major effect on our family routine. We now existed in relation to the burfwala and the daily arrival and destruction of a 20-kilogram block of ice, which became less and less each day as the temperatures rose and bicycle melt rate increased. My wife's earlier indulgence gave way to mild irritation. Weekend trips to the cinema were marred by the rush to get home in time to meet the iceman and load the Snowbreeze. My youngest appeared a little happier, slightly less resentful, but was he really cooler at night? He insisted he was, but it was only after that first summer when temperatures reached 47 °C that it became clear he was telling me what he thought I wanted to hear and didn't have the heart to tell me the cold truth: there was some cooling effect but not enough for a boy raised in the chilly haar of Edinburgh summers.

With this sinking feeling, more questions arose: India is home to one-third of the world's poorest—250 million people live under the international US$ 1.90-a-day poverty line: How many of them could afford to spend ₹6,000 on a Snowbreeze, or buy a fridge-freezer to make the 20 kilograms of ice it required every day for cooling? How many of them could even pay for the electricity it would require? And if not, how many of them could afford the alternative—to buy, as we did, 20 kilograms of ice per day for ₹60 per block?

Snowbreeze economics didn't really stack up for India's very poorest, but even if it did not quite fulfil my hopes, its inventor remained my saviour. He was still in the game, working on improvements, and I received regular updates on new tweaks to improve its cooling capacity, upgraded prototypes exploring the latent heat which improves cooling as ice melts to water.

He had been working on its warming potential too. In the

winter, he replaced the stainless-steel ice buckets with a swinging electric light bulb and turned the Snowbreeze into a low-cost heater.

The contraption itself became smaller and a little neater. Mr Lal was given grants from the government and international manufacturers showed some interest. A company in China started manufacturing them from his open source instruction manual.

I had to concede the Snowbreeze was a much better story than it was an air conditioner but I'd invested in much more than an ugly, semi-cooling contraption. I'd become a stakeholder in Mr Lal's infectious, can-do optimism and a different way of looking at India. Mr Lal had, in fact, opened my eyes to something important and possibly even essential about India which, until now, I'd filed under exotic 'local colour'. I started to see Snowbreeze innovation everywhere I looked.

There were the obvious equivalents on the roads—the half motorbike-half car jugaad trikes that I have mentioned earlier in the book, the Frankenstein's monster of rural public transport and freight. There were farm tractor versions where the motorcycle front was replaced by the front end of a motorized mower. There were rickshaw variants too: half Royal Enfield Bullet attached to a bench seat carriage on scooter wheels covered by a canopy with a glass screen dangling above the handlebars for all-weather vision.

I remembered trucks on the National Highways covered with billowing tarpaulins which made them look like risen tin loaves on wheels but increased their cargo capacity by a third at least.

In the narrow lanes of Old Delhi, bicycles had been sawn in half and welded to steel cages on wheels to make improvised school minibuses for young girls in immaculately pressed uniforms.

Bicycles are, arguably, host to more jugaad innovation than even the Enfield Bullet. I'd seen bikes modified to use the rear wheel rack as a shop: glass vitrines filled with small crispy golgappas, or compartmentalized to display namkeen. Others had display panels welded onto the handlebars to create a mobile tobacconist shop. My favourite had a small grindstone mounted on the crossbar, attached by a fan belt to the rear wheel so the rider could flip the bike up on the kickstand and pedal to sharpen knives from his seat.

In our own colony a baker's boy brought the shop to your doorstep with its rack transformed into both bread bin, store counter and carving board—he sold brown and white bread by the slice. I noticed a jugaad genius in how some hawkers loaded vast stocks of their wares on to their bicycle and still managed to ride it: Hundreds of cheap metal bartan cascading down from the hawkers back, bulging out in every direction, turning him, his bike and the pots into a moving, disco ball. Jharoowalas had turned their bicycles into broom emporia which from the street looked like moving, Day-Glo fluff balls with khus, straw and nylon brushes in pink, yellow and green poking out from every part of the frame.

M. B. Lal's early memories of invention as a preserve of eccentric Americans and Britons were no doubt genuine, but you only needed to gaze at the everyday circus of Indian street life to see a national talent for innovation and improvisation. I was high on hope, inspired by Lal-ji, and I didn't want the feeling to end. I set out to find more like him and dig deeper for the source.

CHAPTER 2

SWADESHI R & D

'To invent, you need a good imagination and a pile of junk.'
—Thomas Edison

In a temporary exhibition tent on the lawn of the Rashtrapati Bhavan, a line of awkward middle-aged men wait nervously in their wedding best, like boys dressed by their mothers, pulling at tight collars and patting down unruly hair as they line up for the stage. They are the nominees for the National Innovation Awards and they are about to be honoured by India's head of state before an audience of cabinet ministers, diplomats, senior government officials and journalists, all seated on white cotton-covered chairs tied at the back with red satin bows.

For these 'frugal innovators' it is a redemption moment and perhaps the greatest day of their lives. They have overcome the most daunting obstacles to be here today: minimal schooling, harsh poverty, caste discrimination, the resentment of families who thought they should spend more time putting food on the table and the ridicule of fellow villagers who said they were crazy.

The occasion is stiff and the nominees are intimidated—these hitherto unsung heroes are rickshaw pullers, farmers and labourers in the company of India's great and good and the ceremony is all the more moving for that: marginalized men starved of recognition or appreciation, finally honoured by their head of state. Today, they are no longer mad pipe-dreamers who waste their days on fantasies while their families go hungry, but are the hope of a rising nation.

The Lifetime Achievement Award goes to Amrutbhai Agrawat, a sixty-eight-year-old serial inventor from Gujarat for his 'Tilting Bullock Cart', which attaches to the beast without cutting its hide and empties its load by compression to save women labourers struggling too long in the sun. The bullock cart is a symbol of backwardness to some Indian patriots who prefer to focus on the country's achievements in automobile design, space exploration and rocket science. They bring traffic to a halt and are often the cause of road accidents—one district administration is even considering new rules to force them to sport luminous strips if they are on the roads at night. Yet they remain central to the lives of millions of farm labourers and Amrutbhai Agrawat believes his invention could help lighten their load.

Amrutbhai began his working life as a child labourer in Malia, in Gujarat's Junagadh district. He left school when his father died and went to work with his mother on a local farm. Today he is a 'serial innovator' who has graduated to a small workshop making farm gates, granary boxes and agricultural machinery. He has sixteen inventions to his name and two of them—a wheat sowing box and groundnut digger—have won several prizes. His most effective invention has not only been life-changing, but life-saving too: a pulley lever which attaches to bucket ropes in village wells. Fetching water is often left to women and children and occasionally, when they forget to let go of the rope, they are pulled into the shaft and plunge to their deaths. Amrutbhai's Ganga Pulley Ratchet is attached to the well wall and stops the rope whenever the person drawing water stops pulling. Apart from saving lives it allows elderly women to pause for breath without dropping the bucket and has prevented rope burns. 'A simple but brilliant idea,' says Professor Anil Gupta, executive vice chairperson of the National Innovation Foundation and founder of the Honey Bee Network which champions India's frugal inventors and folk wisdom.

The award recognizes in Amrutbhai a common trait among

most of these ragged-trousered innovators: their creations are aimed
at improving the lives of India's poorest and hardest-working people
rather than helping themselves get rich quick. Amrutbhai's own
circumstances have improved, but only gradually after decades of
private, self-funded research and development. 'He's slowly made his
way through,' Professor Gupta explains. 'Now has his own house.
He's not very rich but he's okay.'

There is a national award for Gurmail Singh Dhonsi, whose
Rapid Compost Aerator reduces composting time from three months
to just three weeks. Fazlul Hoque from Assam is honoured for his
paddy threshing machine, while Sib Sankar Mandal from Kokrajhar is
recognized for his work to increase fuel mileage in engines. There is
a consolation award for D. N. Venkat's coconut tree-climbing device
designed to ease one of the most hazardous jobs in the tropics—
shinnying up 100 foot-tall branchless palm trees to pick a few heavy
coconuts. It combines two metal frames that grip the tree as the
climber sits in a canvas seat and locks one while raising the other
to scale the trunk. He has sold several hundreds of them throughout
India's palm-growing states and exported them to other Southeast
Asian countries too.

Professor Gupta is their guru and devoted cheerleader who sees
their commitment and talent as the very best of India. His focus
is on how their inventions can be harnessed, developed and shared
for maximum social benefit, rather than which among them will
be first to strike it rich.

A millionaire would however be a milestone for the Honey Bee
Network and he'd be happy for any of the inventors to escape the
poverty most of them live in. His best bet is Dharamveer Kamboj,
a low-caste farmer who worked as a cycle rickshaw puller in Old
Delhi's Khari Baoli spice market, and is a real rags-to-relative-riches
story.

As a young newlywed, Dharamveer fled his father's tiny
smallholding in Haryana's Damla village in fear of local moneylenders.
He had borrowed to pay his late mother's hospital bills but he couldn't

make the payments. He left his young wife and baby daughter and, with just a few rupees and a wedding gift watch, headed for Delhi. He sold the watch to a local wine shop owner for ₹70, spent ₹35 on a bus ticket, and a few hours later he was one of the thousands of young migrants who arrive in the capital every day searching for work. Within days he was a human beast of burden, a cycle rickshaw puller heaving overfed traders and tourists through the Walled City's baked streets by day, and sleeping contorted and exhausted on his trike by night.

It was while taking fruit traders to the Khari Baoli spice market that he first saw the seeds of an idea which would transform him from laughing stock and marked man to the wealthiest and most respected in his village and beyond.

He had overheard traders complaining about the problems they faced in processing amla. He tucked it away and mulled it over when he finally returned to his village eight months later with the cash to repay his creditors.

He had been an indifferent student at school, skipping classes when the going got tough, but he had always been resourceful on the farm. When he was eleven, he had rescued his family from a financial crisis by rebuilding their sugar cane crusher which had been declared irreparable by the mechanic just as they were about to juice a bumper crop.

At thirteen, when electricity became more widely accessible in the village, he created a cheap hotplate with clay plates, discarded oil drums and electric coils. He sold them for ₹12 each to every housewife in his village who preferred them to the 50-rupee factory-made ovens on sale in the market. It is still known in his village as the 'Jugaad Heater'.

'We used a tin box, clay plate and element to make our hotplate and first used it in our homes. Soon, there was huge demand for it in the village. Our hotplate was priced ₹12 and the villagers, particularly women, liked it. Until then they'd had to use firewood to cook but our hotplate made it easy for them to cook instantly,' he said.

When he was seventeen, he made battery-powered emergency lights for his local hospital, which kicked in during power cuts. Unfortunately none of his inventions made the kind of money his family needed to pay their medical bills or keep the moneylenders at bay. He had hoped his skills would help him land a good job in the capital but after two weeks his money was running out fast and he spent his last few rupees on renting a cycle rickshaw.

The life of a cycle rickshawwala in Old Delhi is harsh and punishing. They are too many of them, competition is fierce and fares are low. Often they pedal families of four uphill in 40 °C heat on boiling roads. It is back-breaking work and then there are stick-wielding policemen who slash their tyres and demand bribes. 'The income was meagre and I often lined up outside temples for food brought by devotees. I carried my 10th grade certificate with me all the time, thinking I might meet someone who could give me a job,' he said.

The certificate didn't help, but his knowledge of traditional herbs and spices, which he'd learned from his mother as a child, did. Many of his passengers were fruit processors and dried fruit buyers searching for supplies in the spice market and Dharamveer became a sought-after guide. He sent money home to his family and saved to clear his debt.

A fractured leg from a road accident eventually forced him to return to his village where he was bedridden for four months with plenty of time to think about his future. When he finally emerged he started growing aloe vera in his fields and met government agriculture officials to research processing methods. He joined a government scheme which gave grants of ₹25,000 for farmers to start their own processing plants, but it was only a fraction of the ₹100,000 he needed to buy the processing equipment. He decided to make his own. 'I had examined the machines in Ajmer and Pushkar and decided to use a copper vessel, thinking that if the venture fails I can rent it to villagers for wedding ceremonies,' he said.

He found a roadside steel fabricator and started working on

his design. He fitted grinders, juicers and mixers to the top of the vessel but struggled to build the condenser he needed to process the fruit. After eleven months, the fabricator told him it wasn't working and he couldn't help him any longer. 'I gave him ₹40,000 and took the unfinished machine to my home. For another three months, I worked on it. I was so engaged with it that I often used to skip my meals,' he said.

As the amount of time and money he spent on his machine increased, the patience of his father and wife began to wear thin. In 2005, he was forced to sell his house and a portion of his land to repay bank loans he had taken. 'I was devoting too much time to my creative work. My financial condition was such that I was unable to pay school fees of my children and they were almost shunted out of the school. Many people in my village as well as my relatives thought I was crazy and that I would ruin my life. My family was traumatized by the taunts. It was difficult for them to ignore the jibes and at times they would get angry with me,' he said.

Despite their misgivings Dharamveer refused to give up. 'I had always had this urge to do something different and believed nothing is impossible. I knew I had some special talent. I didn't let it die but worked to find alternate mediums to achieve my goals. Perseverance is important, all great men had been bullied and put down by people around them but they believed in themselves and had their eyes on the goal rather than people who would criticize them,' he explained.

Sixteen months and many tweaks later, his perseverance paid off and he finally unveiled his creation. 'The machine was able to grind, condense, chop, peel, process and mix herbs, vegetables, fruits and it was portable. It saved time and money for small farmers in our village and became an instant hit,' he said.

It had cost him years of toil, ridicule and money he didn't have—₹1,40,000 and eight years—but he started selling it under his own brand name 'Homemade by Kissan Dharambir Damla' and also established his own processing business extracting rose water, grinding aloe vera into gel and peeling garlic. The machine makes jams, purees and ketchup which he sells under the brand name 'Prince' after his son, an IT graduate who now works in the family business.

His work and the story of his rise from Old Delhi rickshawwala to a pioneering village entrepreneur was reported in local newspapers and the coverage brought new recognition and funding. In 2006, the Asia Entrepreneurs' Conference gave him ₹60,000 to improve his machine further, and in the same year he won India's National Award for Grassroots Innovation.

Since then he has sold his machines throughout India and Africa too. He is not quite a dollar millionaire but he is a crorepati—a rupee millionaire—and now an industrialist who employs many of the same villagers who once mocked him as a mad loser.

◆

The road to his village in Yamunanagar, Haryana, is slow. There are herds of cows, muddy black bullocks with downturned horns. We pass unrendered red brick houses with barely any cement to hold them together. In front of his sprawling complex of workshops and living rooms, there are dozens of motorbikes and cars on either side of a pink and gold pandal festooned with marigolds. A red carpet on green baize passes through the portal and Dharamveer is here to greet me. It is his son's wedding and a big day for the Kamboj family, another milestone in their journey from the misery of ridicule to the celebration of success and the respect and sycophancy that accompanies it. He is standing, hand outstretched, in dark slacks, a grey, open-necked shirt, his white hair and greying moustache neatly combed, beaming with pride. He ushers me first into a room where his wife, Shyamudevi, and the women of the family are sitting cross-legged, singing and clapping, their pastel saris flapping in time and their wrists, heavy with jingling jewellery, joining the percussion. Inside, the walls are decked with pictures of Dharamveer being 'felicitated' by India's great and good. It's a very nice house for a man who once worked as human transport in Old Delhi's spice market. A portrait of India's then trade minister, Anand Sharma, clasping Dharamveer's hands, has pride of place.

We walk through a workshop containing his chrome fruit pulping and processing machines, another room where his early prototypes are stored and into the rear garden where a large wedding tent has been erected with beige curtains, red drapes and green carpets. Dharamveer is the centre of attention, the host of the grand feast, surrounded by well-wishers and officials who want to be associated with his success story. Bollywood disco music is blaring, children are topping up on Coke, and a line has formed on the bumpy baize for the buffet lunch.

Dharamveer's daughter Pooja, in a rose pink embroidered tulle sari, glittering with gold and jewels, takes me aside to tell me what all this means to their family. Her brother's union is a 'love marriage' with a girl from their Kamboj sub-caste—a low, peasant caste of tilling smallholders. 'Love marriages' are discouraged in rural Haryana and occasionally end in so-called honour killings, but it is a mark of the respect Dharamveer commands that the wedding is well-attended by the local elite. 'Because he had no education, people are surprised. They did not think the function could be like this. They expect not much showing, a simple wedding, not a big arrangement. People didn't like to talk to us. People called my father pagal. They thought he wasn't doing any earning, family members did not like him because he was not interested in traditional agriculture. He wanted to do something new. The family was against this.

'They never laughed in front of us, but in their homes or villages maybe, behind our backs,' she said.

Today, his daughter is studying for her MBA degree, the family owns three motorbikes and Dharamveer is about to buy a Toyota Innova car. The villagers are now laughing with him. His jugaad way of thinking which once brought derision is now a source of local wealth and he is quick to acknowledge it. 'Jugaad is an idea, to make a device not available in the market to meet more needs. I look in my surroundings for things, I assemble them to create a device which helps me undertake things which are not otherwise possible. I pick cheap things, things not useful to others to make that device.

'I had acumen for innovations right from my childhood. During my schooldays, I wasn't academically that brilliant but I had great desire to create new things. I devised my first gadget at the age of twelve. It was 1975 and as a student I used to skip my classes and work on the gadget in sugar cane fields along with my friend. Right from my first gadget I tried to use simple and easily available items which would be used in place of regular machines. These were jugaads, innovations, but with time I have been developing proper machinery, developed after thorough research and ideation. India being a vast country with half of the population still struggling with poverty and illiteracy, it is important to develop devices which are cheap, easy to use and can be a substitute for standard gadgets,' he explained.

His aim isn't sophistication, which would be beyond the pockets of his target market—poor and lower middle-class people like himself. 'Sophisticated gadgets are costly and out of reach for many people. My aim is always to make devices which are within the reach of common people across the world. My gadgets are exported to all Indian states and foreign countries like Kenya. I think these devices ought to be crude to make them affordable for people. We do not compare them with standard machines but at times they are more efficient,' he said.

◆

Dharamveer's work has been championed by Professor Gupta's Honey Bee Network which collects, cross-pollinates and develops ideas from India's frugal inventors to help them harvest the fruits of their labour. So far they have collated 1,50,000 ideas, filed 500 patents of which thirty-five have been granted in India and four in the United States, and registered sixty-four technology licenses. Neither Professor Gupta nor his staff like the word jugaad. They believe it belittles scientific research conducted by frugal innovators and restricts their access to the capital they need to develop their ideas.

The imagination and determination required and the painstaking research and development they do is no less than any done in wealthy research institutes, they argue. Its advantage is in the uplifting altruism behind each project—these innovators are usually more socially than financially motivated.

Forty-two-year-old Nathubhai Vadha from Surendranagar in Gujarat is a good example. He, like many in his district, three hours from Ahmedabad, is a struggling cotton farmer, and although he has 22 acres, they are as much a burden as a boon. His trousers are polyester and he is wearing plastic sandals. Every year in March and April he needs 200 cotton pickers to bring in the harvest but labourers are increasingly difficult to find, so he began exploring mechanical solutions. He had been interested in machines as a child but had never made anything in his life. His idea took shape when he noticed how the vibration of his tractor engine alone made cotton balls fall to the ground as he drove by. 'I realized that picking is not difficult. The need is for a mechanism to collect the fallen balls. So I developed two platforms on both sides of the tractor furrows to collect the balls,' he explained. The vibration knocks the balls from the plants on to the side platforms and a suction pipe sweeps them into a storage container. His invention is now 90 per cent ready, he said, and will soon be sold as a tractor accessory that could revolutionize Indian cotton farming.

He lives a simple life with his wife, thirteen-year-old daughter, twenty-one-year-old son and his parents. 'I get about ₹1 lakh per year profit. I have a motorcycle, a TV and fridge. I'm satisfied with my standard of living, but more than money I'm interested in creating something I can leave behind that can help other people,' he said.

The exhibition tent next to the Innovation Awards stage is a circus of weird and wonderful contraptions being demonstrated by their proud but modest inventors. Arvind Patel, a fifty-nine-year old mechanic from Gujarat, is explaining his water-cooling system in which steel storage tanks are tightly bound in coir rope which is kept wet by a steady stream of water. A solar-powered fan blows over the wet coir and cools the water inside by evaporation. It reminds me of M. B. Lal's Snowbreeze and his social mission. Like Dharamveer, his idea and the money necessary to develop it had caused hardship for his wife and children and brought ridicule from neighbours. At one point he had been forced to sell his beloved workshop to survive and his wife begged him to give up this 'madness', but he persevered and is today selling his systems throughout India.

On the lawn outside the tent, Assamese rice farmers Mehter Hussain and Mushtaq Ahmed are demonstrating their bamboo windmill and pump which has transformed their lives and those of salt pan workers in the Little Rann of Kutch on Gujarat's Arabian Sea coast. They had built a drag windmill from local bamboo when the cost of renting a diesel pump hit their pockets. The bamboo blades turn a crank shaft which operates the pump and draws 3,000 litres of water per hour in wind speeds of 15 kph. It cost them ₹5,000 to make and saved their livelihoods. In some parts of India farmers sink into debt because of the high cost of renting machinery like pumps and generators. The Honey Bee Network linked the brothers to salt pan workers who needed to draw 80,000 litres per day—the work of two, free to run ₹5,000 bamboo windmills.

But perhaps the most selfless among these frugal innovators is Arunachalam Muruganantham, the Tamil 'tampon king' whose research and development provoked not only ridicule but anger too. He invented his own super-low cost sanitary towels after he realized his wife and other women in his village collected dirty rags to make pads for their periods because they couldn't afford expensive Western pads. 'If I buy sanitary napkins it means I cannot afford to buy milk for the family,' she'd told him.

Western pads cost more than ₹8 each—₹70 for a packet of eight—more than a day's income for many and beyond the reach of 210 million poor rural Indian women who need them. It is the reason why only 12 per cent of India's women use sanitary towels. Yet the lack of modern sanitary protection and abiding taboo means teenage girls miss fifty days of school every year and the number of working days lost for women costs the Indian economy an estimated $15 billion per year.

Arunachalam experimented with cheap local materials to replicate the absorbency of Western sanitary napkins and developed his own pad made of wood pulp wrapped in two layers of polypropylene fabric glued together with non-stick paper. His Laadli or 'Beloved Daughter' brand pads are sold for ₹2 apiece. To develop his revolutionary pad, he collected soiled pads from local medical students to examine their absorbency and tested the quality of his own prototypes on himself, wearing pierced football bladders filled with pigs' blood to replicate menstrual bleeding. The eccentricity of his research embarrassed his family and angered neighbours. Today, however, his pads are on sale throughout rural India and has made life easier for thousands of women.

Perhaps the most successful swadeshi innovation in the last fifty years has been the Jaipur Foot, the prosthetic limb designed in 1968 by artist and sculptor Ram Chandra Sharma. He'd been inspired while teaching art to polio patients in the 'Pink City's' Sawai Man Singh Hospital. India then had the highest number of polio victims in the world with 1.5 lakh new cases every year. The country finally became polio-free in March 2014 but many of the wretched souls with withered limbs seen begging at traffic lights throughout India today are a legacy of that period.

Sharma noticed that imported prosthetics were as unaffordable to the victims as they were uncomfortable to wear, and set out to create an artificial limb more suited to rugged Indian village conditions.

He took a plaster mould of an amputee's stump to make an exact-fit plug covered in High Density Polyethylene Pipe, a vulcanized rubber foot was attached to the wood and aluminium limb, and the new limb was strapped to the patient within a day or two. The Jaipur Foot could be worn with shoes, but its lightness, flexibility and strength meant its owners could go barefoot and reclaim the village life their injury had denied them. They could squat in paddy fields, climb trees and ride a bicycle. Western prosthetics had priced this rehabilitation at ₹6 lakh while today state-of-the-art limbs can cost as much as ₹60 lakh in Britain. In Jaipur, a return to normal working life costs a little more than ₹2,000. To date, the Bhagwan Mahaveer Viklang Sahayata Samiti associated with Sharma's invention has treated more than 1.3 million patients around the world including landmine and polio victims in clinics throughout Asia, Africa and South America.

◆

Arunachalam Muruganantham, Amrutbhai Agrawat, Dharamveer Kamboj, M. B. Lal, Ram Chandra Sharma and all these other jugaad inventors and frugal innovators highlight a caring, selfless side of the country motivated by ideas of community and service. But they are much more than that. A homespun thread ties them to some of the great thinkers of India's Swadeshi and Independence movements to—Aurobindo Ghose, who went on to become one of India's great spiritual leaders; Bal Gangadhar Tilak, who led the boycott of British goods in favour of home-made and home rule, and Mahatma Gandhi, the father of the nation.

They are swadeshis, ambassadors for the Indian philosophy of self-reliance and vision of how India should be: A country which depends on its own ancient civilization, resources and creative genius to meet its needs; one which rejects a global economy based on exploitation and the elevation of material wealth above spiritual peace. Gandhi's swadeshi politics and philosophy was symbolized by the charkha he used to spin his own khadi cloth in protest at the dumping of cotton from Manchester's mills on India. For Gandhi, the charkha was an enduring reminder of India's historic economic independence and the wholesome village self-sufficiency he envisaged for independent India's economic future.

Gandhi's charkha was the centre of village life and the village was at the heart of an Indian ideal in which local is always best. He summed up the swadeshi outlook as a spirit of self-reliance which 'restricts us to the use and service of our immediate surroundings to the exclusion of the more remote'. It meant remaining loyal to one's ancestral religion, indigenous political institutions and only using 'things that are produced by my immediate neighbours'.

Their swadeshi roots connect our frugal innovators to some of post-independence India's most significant leaders, from Gandhian socialists like Ram Manohar Lohia who inspired India's non-Congress opposition, to Jayaprakash Narayan whose national protest movement against Indira Gandhi's authoritarianism was squashed by her imposition of the Emergency. The end of the Emergency saw the rise of Narayan's followers in the Janata Party which won the general election to become India's first non-Congress party to come to power. Narayan's followers included some of the defining political figures of recent decades, among them powerful regional leaders like Nitish Kumar and Lalu Prasad Yadav in Bihar and Mulayam Singh Yadav in Uttar Pradesh.

Narayan was a passionate supporter of the British economist Fritz Schumacher, whose book *Small is Beautiful* inspired the global environmentalist movement. It is a manifesto against industrial mass production, which he regarded as 'inherently violent' and inhumane. He believed it led to rural depopulation, urbanization and mass unemployment. Instead, he promoted sustainable 'intermediate technology', which he described as an advance on primitive technologies but 'simpler, cheaper, and freer than the super-technology of the rich'. Man, he said, is small, and 'small is beautiful'.

His book featured a picture of Mahatma Gandhi on its cover and inspired 'appropriate technology' institutes in Varanasi and Lucknow. Chaudhary Charan Singh, the Janata Party prime minister, was said to carry a copy of Schumacher's book with him as constant inspiration.

Their ideas also found an echo on the Hindu nationalist right of Indian politics, including the Rashtriya Swayamsevak Sangh (RSS), linked to the BJP. I spoke to K. N. Govindacharya, a former general secretary of the BJP. Senior BJP leader Ram Madhav told me I needed to meet him if I really wanted to understand swadeshi thinking.

I found him in suitably humble surroundings—a small local authority-built duplex flat in South Delhi's middle-class Vasant Kunj colony, where he greeted me in white pyjamas and a saffron tilak on his forehead. He showed me to a table where we talked as he ate breakfast poha—flattened rice and peas.

Swadeshi, he explained, is not simply the favouring of Indian, home-made products over foreign, but a complete rejection of Western materialism and its 'Protestant-inspired social contract theory'. It is a spiritual understanding of economics and Man's place in nature and society.

'Eat, drink and be merry and then die cannot be the goal of life. Something beyond this has to be the goal of life. This is the Bharatiya understanding. Something transcends.

'There is an interconnectivity between Jeeva (the individual), Jagadisha (the Almighty) and Jagat (our existence in the world) which determines the Indian understanding of life and its goals—simplicity, non-materialism and a recognition that Man is part of nature and not conqueror of nature. Indians live in a relationship-based society, not one in which the individual comes first,' he said. It is a 'let live, then live' philosophy in which the 'acquiring, accumulating and showing of wealth is a criminal act'.

In the West where individual rights are promoted over social responsibilities, 'technology evolved which had no qualms or agitation in damaging nature' and Man had become a 'super-predator' pursuing 'eco-destructive economics and politics,' he explained.

I had knocked on Govindacharya's door expecting to meet a right-wing hardliner in khaki shorts but instead found a man whose views would find a supportive audience among left-wing environmentalists and anarchists anywhere in Europe. He was more tree-hugger than goose-stepper with loud echoes of Gandhi and Schumacher in his thoughts. Above all he believes India must organize its economy in accordance with its own cultural beliefs and produce goods which meet its unique needs and circumstances.

In his exposed-brick office at the Indian Institute of Management in Ahmedabad, Gujarat, Professor Anil Gupta is explaining his philosophy to colleagues in his Honey Bee Network. In a pale blue kurta which highlights his salt-and-pepper beard, he has the air of a guru as much as an academic.

Swadeshi, frugal innovators like Dharamveer Kamboj, M. B. Lal and Ram Chandra Sharma, he believes, are not only the best of India but keepers of a folk tradition which has been ignored and wasted. In them he sees infinite potential and wants the country's leaders to tap into it. They represent a vision of how India could be.

His earliest memories are from his childhood in Old Delhi's Daryaganj where he slept with thirteen relatives in a small room and everything which could be reused was saved and recycled.

'When we went to market we would put the things in newspapers and wrap them in twine. My uncle took the things out of the paper, spread it on the bed and hung the thread on a nail so next time we needed to give something to someone we could use the paper and thread. Even that was not thrown out. We have lived with that frugality. Society respects people who are frugal, who don't show off their wealth. People worth a lot of money in Gujarat don't show it off,' he says, drawing a contrast with the ostentation he sees in Delhi.

His identification with the innovative poor and his fascination with its frugal folk wisdom followed an epiphany. In 1980, he was researching the impact of drought during a stint at Delhi's Indian Institute of Public Administration. He met a farmer who had discovered he could predict the success of his harvest by studying the pattern of weeds in his fields. 'This farmer started telling me that when you have these weed flows it gives him an indication of how his crop will perform. He knew he would get a better crop by looking at the weed flow. He was forecasting the climate by looking at the behaviour of weeds which sense changes in the weather in advance,' he said. He was as amazed by the potential of the discovery as its source. 'My God, there is knowledge here and it is not from labs,' he said. In 1984, while studying new crop varieties, he discovered that poor farmers preferred growing taller millet with a higher straw-to-grain ratio. When he asked why, they told him their livestock help them survive the drought months, so they needed more straw for fodder. 'They needed food even when there was no grain to survive the dry period—something scientists had missed,' he said.

These discoveries opened his eyes to a world of knowledge few scientists and researchers had bothered to consider. But now he'd noticed it, he started to look closer.

He was invited to Bangladesh by President Hussain Muhammad Ershad to advise its government on how to focus its agriculture policies on the poor, and while there found another untapped reservoir of discoveries. In Rangpur, he saw farmers planting areca palm for betel nuts in a circle around banana trees which store water in the monsoon months and release it into the ground during the dry season. He heard reports of tomatoes being sold out of season and found farmers in one village were harvesting them early and hanging the plants upside down to keep them fresh. 'The farmers said they harvest before the tomatoes are ripe, hang the whole plant upside down, they take longer to mature, the chemical ethylene moves slowly that way,' he explained.

In Tangail, famous for its saris, he met a woman trimming all but two of the roots from sweet potatoes. When asked why, she said with fewer roots, the sweet potato skin thickens which means it can be stored for longer. 'She had developed a system for storing potatoes,' he said.

In another area he found poor farmers who ate only one meal a day growing two different varieties of rice, one of them because it took longer to digest. 'The poor are negotiating not just the food but the pangs of hunger. I don't know how many scientists knew about this. If you can make the food last longer in the stomach you can work for longer. As a student of development, [I realized] being poor did not mean intellectually poor. That was the turning point,' he said. He made a point of talking to villagers wherever he went to ask who was doing things differently and began collecting not only local farming folk knowledge but also rural inventors.

These days, the inventors find him, many of them when he makes his biennial shodh yatra or voyage of discovery deep into rural India to uncover its hidden knowledge. His mission is to make sure India doesn't waste its indigenous knowledge and the frugal genius of its swadeshi innovators.

CHAPTER 3

CROREPATIS: THE JUGAAD
GUIDE TO MAKING BILLIONS

K. K. Modi is a billionaire, a crorepati many times over but he'd like to be richer still. He loves the caper of business and sees much merit in jugaad. Over the course of his career he has resorted to jugaad numerous times. His solutions may not be perfect, but he has no doubt that whatever the challenge or circumstance, he will always find a way through. His business methods may differ from Messrs Lal, Muruganantham and Kamboj, but the same jugaad outlook drives him on: an almost American can-do optimism and self-belief, a never-say-die determination to succeed against daunting odds and a fleetness of foot which makes them eternally flexible in the quest for a solution. K. K. Modi believes those qualities are not only the secret of his success but the raw spirit which makes Indian businesses throughout the world survive and prosper where others might fail. It partly explains why two of Britain's top four billionaires are Indian—the Hinduja brothers and the world's biggest steel magnate Lakshmi Niwas Mittal.

I'd seen this spirit as a boy in London in the late 1960s and early 1970s when Indian immigrants, many of whom had arrived in Britain with little more than the clothes they were wearing, began buying local newsagent shops and tobacconists and transforming them into grocery stores with product lines to rival supermarkets. They were seen as ferociously hardworking and resourceful people whose way of working had a marked impact on Britain's social life—people came to expect newsagents and corner shops to be open all hours and to stock fresh bread, milk, beer, tomato ketchup and toys as well as newspapers, sweets and cigarettes. That they were so successful and eventually came to dominate the sector in the face of fierce racial discrimination at that time reveals the determination, toughness and flexibility K. K. Modi believes to be Indian traits and the mark of every jugaadi.

Those qualities have made him and his family one of India's wealthiest, and today his empire includes one of India's largest tobacco companies, Godfrey Phillips, and ranges from agricultural pesticides, cosmetics and fashion textiles to education, restaurants and healthcare. He has instilled the same jugaad outlook in his controversial son Lalit, who hit the cricket world for a six when he established the IPL T20 (Indian Premier League Twenty20) series, a property which is currently valued at ₹34,000 crore. But Lalit Modi himself was banned from the BCCI over alleged impropriety in 2013—a claim he strongly denies.

K. K. Modi was born into considerable wealth—the family has its own company town, Modinagar, around 60 kilometres north of Delhi where their fortune began with a sugar mill. They had long been suppliers to British army cantonments throughout northern India and into what lies today in Pakistan. But as the eldest son of tycoon Rai Bahadur Gujarmal Modi, he was expected to prove his mettle as a moneymaker and from his first forays his father and uncles watched him closely to see if he was worthy of further investment in the future.

His career-defining moment came in 1979, just after he bought a stake in the international tobacco giant Philip Morris' Indian subsidiary, Godfrey Phillips. It seemed he'd made a terrible mistake. Philip Morris had warned him it didn't believe the subsidiary could survive, but his confidence in his own ability was so great that even though he knew nothing about the tobacco industry and hadn't commissioned a due diligence report on the company's problems, he simply couldn't accept it was beyond his ability to revive it. 'They'd used all types of managers and brought everybody and said ki they have to shut it down, because the business has failed here. Now, I have never owned a cigarette company, how do I make it work? So when I bought it I didn't know what the problem was. I will find a way to succeed! Problem is not known, how to fix not known. I am buying and I will fix it! I will find a solution,' he said.

He was a 'jugaad person', he explained, who would find a solution by any means necessary. After completing the deal, he toured the factory floor expecting an answer to leap out at him from its rolling machines, but the manager shot down every suggestion he made. 'He said he had been there running twenty years, "all these suggestions you are making, all of these things we have already considered and ruled out, what is the use of reconsidering? If the solution was so easy as what you are saying, Philip Morris would have found, they know the cigarette business".' When the tour ended, K. K. Modi told the manager he was fired and paid up his five-year contract. 'I told mister "goodbye"', he said.

He'd just bought a failing business without doing the necessary research, sacked the one man who knew the factory better than anyone and was now living entirely on his wits. He was, however, relieved to be rid of his manager's grim realism and happy to be alone with his cascading self-confidence.

'There was a person who was the finance guy, Mr Nayar, he was following me...he said "Mr Modi, you don't understand, in four days we have to pay salary, but there is no money to pay salary." So we sat down and looked at accounts receivable. Do we have any saleable assets? He said "whatever assets were there before, Philip Morris has already sold. You may be able to buy five, six days more, by paying the suppliers late but we have to find money. Philip Morris weren't able to bring money, so you bring money!" I said I don't have any money, whatever money I had I have invested to buy Philip Morris here. Now what do we do?' he said.

As he and his advisers crawled over the company books, they

found their former manager's analysis and Philip Morris' warning had been broadly correct: there was no obvious answer to its problems, and on paper the company did indeed appear to be doomed. The jugaadi entrepreneur's starting point however isn't the bleak warning and attendant dark pessimism, but blind faith that a solution is possible and boundless optimism that its discovery is imminent.

For K. K. Modi and his Godfrey Phillips pup, even imminent may have been too late and financial ruin seemed unavoidable.

'We had to come up with something nobody had thought about. We looked at the whole profit and loss account and saw where the cash is going—most of the money we are recovering is going to pay things, raw materials, suppliers, packing, salaries, electricity, excise duty. Even if we get 5 or 10 per cent efficiency, that is not going to solve the problem. Can we stop the excise duty? No, Philip Morris will not permit us to do anything illegal. I said I don't want to go to jail. How do I get money?

'Now we have to revive, we don't know how we will revive, we don't know what we will do. But we will do unusual things because all usual things have already been tried. A jugaad person can't explain how it will be done but he will try many things and one of them will work,' he explained.

Without a quick fix to pay the monthly salary bill, the question of solving the company's deeper malaise was academic. One way was to stop paying taxes, use these funds to pay salaries and hope to survive long enough to set things right later. But how could he dodge the taxman without courting arrest? He met his lawyer in Mumbai and told him he needed an arguable case to withhold the payments.

They found a tiny loophole in the law, crafted an argument that the rate at which they were paying tax was wrong and then flew to Hong Kong to persuade the international parent company, Philip Morris, that their case was solid. '[Their] lawyers and accountants studied it and said this explanation is flyable,' he said. The ruse saved enough money to pay the salary bill and it kept the taxman at bay for six months before the government changed the law, retroactively, to close the loophole and demand the payments he'd withheld. By then, though, he'd increased cigarette sales, improved the factory's efficiency and he paid the tax in six instalments over the following year. The company went on to become India's second largest cigarette firm.

K. K. Modi had survived by the seat of his pants and he throws his head back with a gravelly laugh as he rounds off the story. He is a consummate risk-taker and he takes a great pride in it. But where did it come from? What possessed him to sink his money into a business without knowing the scale of its liabilities and problems? Where did he acquire the confidence to believe he could triumph in any circumstances? The answer, he said, is in one of his earliest memories from his childhood, a family wedding at his home in Modinagar. As the preparations hurtled towards the big day, a sudden shortage of milk threatened disaster: a celebration without sweets. No traditional laddus would have meant lasting shame for the Modis when thousands of guests arrived just two days later. His father sent for Sadhu Ram, the manager of their sugar cane factory, and told him he had two days to find hundreds of gallons of milk. The manager, without any knowledge of local dairy farming, told him not to worry, he'd deliver. 'At that time he didn't know how to get the milk. Several hundred—perhaps a thousand—guests are coming; it was a time of shortage,' he explained.

Sadhu Ram set his staff to work tracing every nearby cow owner and discovered that all the farmers who sold sugar cane to the factory also kept a cow for milk for their families. He struck a deal with each to buy all their cows' milk over the next three days and saved the Modis from years of humiliation.

'There are two types of managers, those who can't do it and others who can do it. They may not be using the best solution, but that is the solution available. And nobody else can do it. My mother said there was a problem, so many guests are coming, so much milk, can you organize it? The manager at that time doesn't know. But if he promises, he delivers. That creates the need of jugaad. I [learned] that there are people who can promise you and deliver,' he said.

His son Lalit had been in a similar situation in 2009, when the Congress-led government asked him to delay the second season of his IPL T20 cricket series. The country was still recovering from the devastating terrorist attack on Mumbai in November the previous year when more than 160 people were killed in a three-day rampage by gunmen from Pakistan. The threat to cricket was highlighted by the attack by terrorist gunmen on the Sri Lankan cricket team on their way to Lahore's Gaddafi Stadium a few weeks earlier, killing seven people (six of them policemen) and injuring nearly twenty (including seven Sri Lankan players). The tournament clashed with the Indian general elections and the government could not spare the security forces necessary to protect both. Elections versus cricket would be a nail-biting match in any Indian's heart, but there could be only one winner—IPL 2 would have to be delayed, cancelled or relocated. 'I don't want my forces being stretched... [after the elections] would be a better proposition,' then Home Minister P. Chidambaram said.

For Modi Jnr, cancellation wasn't an option and delay would have taken the tournament into the cauldron of the Indian summer. He decided he would shift the entire tournament—fifty-nine matches in eight cities over forty-five days—to South Africa instead and honour its broadcasting commitments. The logistical challenge of moving the teams, coaches, marketing departments, some of the world's best and highest paid cricketers, across continents and finding venues, hotels would be daunting to most executives, but not to a jugaadi.

'When Lalit created IPL, he promises big things and then he looks at how to deliver it,' his father explained.

Not the other way around?

'No! Other way you can't—in two weeks I have to transfer all the matches from here to South Africa. How did he do it? He knew there was a guy who was the head of Disney entertainment. First, he hired him. Next two weeks we have to do it, you come on board. Then he hired IMG [International Management Group] in time to implement. Organizing a tournament, going to a new government where I don't know anyone, where there is huge bureaucracy. How to do it? There was a guy who owned the stadiums, Mr Gupta, Indian guy. He told him I'm going to hold six matches, I'll use your stadium. But I will need all the approvals.

'Nobody could do it because there was no example to shift to another continent in two weeks, conducted without any glitch. He got it from "if a promise is made then it has to be kept". He didn't know but he had no doubt in his mind that he could find a way. It comes from the Indian companies, when they buy a company, they buy because the foreigners running the company are making a loss. Indian guy goes and says I will buy. He doesn't know at that time how he will fix it... We don't do due diligence,' he explained.

It was from K. K. Modi that I first heard the word jugaad in 2010 when I interviewed him as Britain's recently-elected prime minister David Cameron was on his way to India, hoping to win a slice of what was then a remarkable growth story. The sun was setting on Britain as it headed for recession, but was rising fast in India where growth rates were still nudging 9 per cent.

K. K. explained that the secret of India's success was its resilient, resourceful managers, who always find a way through, no matter the obstacle. 'Corruption is too much, roads are bad and there are a lot of negatives. You have to succeed in spite of these problems,' he said.

British bosses were reliable and honest, but not tough enough to thrive in India. They needed to learn from Indian managers, they needed to adopt jugaad, which he explained was a Hindi word meaning 'to fix things so life can continue, though not necessarily through the best solution'. It was, he said, the essential 'character of the Indian manager'. There is a 'flexibility' in Indian managers 'to find a solution that does not go by the book' which had led them to become chief executives of some of the world's biggest companies, he said. British managers were dependable but high maintenance and pampered. 'They deliver what they promise, but they will not do the job in conditions an Indian will accept,' he said.

Some of India's most successful entrepreneurs had made and increased their fortunes because of their jugaad outlook, he said. Lakshmi Mittal's business career took off when he ignored his father's instructions to sell off the land intended for a steel plant in Indonesia and decided to press ahead anyway. 'He didn't know how to fix a steel mill, so he was clever, he thought ki "Okay, public sector in India has good engineers, I will bring them and they will fix the machines." And they did, he made the operation in Indonesia successful,' he said. It was his first step to becoming the world's largest steel manufacturer and one of the world's richest men.

K. K. recounted swapping similar tales with the Hinduja brothers, who succeeded Lakshmi Mittal as Britain's richest billionaires. They had drawn on their jugaad instincts when the Shah of Iran had approached them in the 1970s to help him solve a potato and onion shortage which had caused prices to soar. The Hindujas discovered that while Iran faced a potato and onion crisis, farmers in India's Punjab, 1,200 kilometres to the east, were struggling to cope with a glut which had slashed prices and left them with thousands of tonnes of potatoes which would soon rot unsold—so near and yet so far. Pakistan at that time did not allow overland trade between Iran and India, the Partition enemy it had fought three wars against, the last only a few years earlier.

However, as Indian traders with roots in Pakistan's Sindh province, the Modis had maintained good links with its political leaders. They spoke to the then prime minister, Indira Gandhi, and Zulfikar Ali Bhutto, her Pakistani counterpart, and worked out a historic deal. When it was thwarted at the last minute, the Hindujas needed all the jugaad they could muster to fulfil their promise to the Shah.

K. K. Modi cannot think of an Indian tycoon who is not also a jugaadi, but he reserves special praise for its ultimate practitioner, the late Dhirubhai Ambani, the 'Polyester Prince' who rose from a humble petrol pump attendant in Aden to become India's most powerful and one of the world's richest men. 'Dhirubhai Ambani, maximum jugaad!' he exclaimed in a reverie of deep admiration.

Dhirubhai Ambani made his first fortune after he discovered silver rials from the neighbouring Arab kingdom of Yemen were worth more in London's bullion market than as local currency. He put out an open-ended offer in the souks, melted them down in Aden and sold the silver at a profit in London. With this first fortune he returned to Mumbai where in the early 1960s he set himself up as a yarn trader.

K. K. Modi was introduced to him as a potential buyer when his Modi Mills in Modinagar found itself lumbered with stocks of rayon suit fabric it couldn't sell. He had promised his father he would begin making rayon suits to compete with rival Gwalior Rayon, owned by the wealthy Birla family, and had imported large consignments of yarn in expectation of vast orders which never materialized. To break even he offered to sell the yarn to Gwalior at a discount but they declined, hoping to teach the rival Modis a lesson. K. K. Modi had promised his father great profits but instead was looking at heavy losses, not least in face.

In desperation, he asked his Mumbai agent to sound out local contacts and offer the stock at a 10 per cent discount. He called back later and said a yarn trader, Dhirubhai Ambani, had offered to buy the entire stock but insisted on meeting the owner first.

When they met, Dhirubhai Ambani fired a series of questions at his prospective supplier to soften him up for an even better deal. 'Sir, I don't know what kind of businessman you are. Have you imported this to make loss or profit?' he asked. He was not interested in trading with anyone happy to make a loss. 'He said so how much profit do you want to make? Question of loss does not arise. I will buy from you for profit, I would not like to deal with you if there is no profit. I said okay. I agree. '5 or 10 per cent,' he said.

Then, as they were about to shake hands on the deal, the yarn trader revealed he could not pay. 'He said: "Sir I have no money." He had no money! I said "Dhirubhai, if you have no money, how will you sell my yarn?" He said "that's not your worry. But if I can't sell, I will give you the money with interest. And take the deliveries starting from one month from now, so your loss is covered and your profit is there, but once we shake the hand you can't sell to anyone else." Normally you don't agree to this type of thing, no advance, nothing, by word. But that looked serious to me because my yarn was not selling at any price.'

He didn't dare tell his father of his high-risk deal but a month later he got a call from rivals Gwalior Rayon to say they'd had a problem with their fabric and they would like to buy his yarn after all.

'I said material is with me but I've already sold it, now if you want to buy you have to go to Dhirubhai. Dhirubhai added his own profit on top of that and paid me the money with interest,' he said with a roar of laughter.

'Now somehow or the other he did something or luck smiled on him, the lot of Gwalior failed... [their own] yarn did not run in warp... He found a solution. Everything is not mechanical. Jugaad means you create a solution of a problem that is not solvable at that moment. And if you corrected that, you beat the emergency situation,' he explained.

K. K. Modi would gladly tell his jugaad business stories for the rest of his life. And I'd gladly listen to them, but I was a little sceptical. Indian businessmen, it seemed then, were taking over the crumbling Western economy. The Tatas had bought Jaguar Land Rover, they owned Britain's biggest steel producer Corus and were now the country's biggest employer. Controversial liquor baron Vijay Mallya, who later fled the country, had used his vast beer-and-whisky-to-airlines-and-sport empire to buy Whyte & Mackay, one of Scotland's largest distillers. Subrata Roy, the so-called Managing Worker and Chairman of the Sahara India Pariwar, who made his vast fortune persuading poor farmers to invest a rupee or two every month in his 'parabanking' savings scheme, had bought London's Grosvenor House Hotel. As Britain's fortunes waned, Indian billionaires were taking over in a 'reverse Raj' and London had become 'the new Shimla', a cool climate resort to which Mumbai and Bengaluru-based tycoons could flit in summer to show off their riches and acquire a few more companies.

Could all that success really be founded on cutting corners and beating the system? The sheer scale of their multibillion-dollar takeovers required finance. Banks don't lend large amounts without a thorough investigation into who's asking and what they plan to do with the loan.

I called Gopichand Hinduja, one of the two brothers who run the family's vast financial empire which spans banks to trucks, oil to cable television and digital media, and asked if he could explain the role jugaad had played in their own rise. I'd met the brothers shortly after we moved to Delhi in 2005 through a political fixer. They were accused and later acquitted by the courts in the Bofors corruption scandal, in which kickbacks were said to have been paid on a deal to buy howitzer field guns. His style of entrepreneurship seemed very different from K. K. Modi's—business decisions were more calculated and based on an understanding of the political landscape of the countries in question and their relationship with its decision makers. The Hindujas analyse, collect market intelligence and plan strategically. They did not quite seem to be the jugaadis K. K. Modi had admiringly described.

The family business was started by their father Parmanand in Shikarpur, Sindh, in today's Pakistan, and moved first to Mumbai, as it was then, in 1914, and later in 1919 to Iran. They sold Persian dried fruits to India and Indian tea, jute, textiles and sugar in the other direction. Parmanand taught his sons to never miss opportunities and when he died in 1971, they transformed the $4 million estate he left them, which included just $1 million in cash and property in Iran worth $3 million, into one of the world's largest trading empires. Today, their combined wealth is estimated at around $19 billion. In one of their most successful early deals they bought the international film rights to Raj Kapoor's 1964 Bollywood romance *Sangam*, a tale of secret love, self-denial, friendship and betrayal. They reportedly paid ₹13 lakh for it, dubbed it into Persian and released it in Iran where it was a huge hit, netting great box office profits.

Relaxing on a sofa in the family's New Zealand House office in London's Haymarket, looking out over the Millennium Eye on the South Bank of the Thames, Gopichand Hinduja explained that 'jugaadism' is an important aspect of entrepreneurialism. 'Jugaadism in my view can only come into entrepreneurs, who never accept no, they always try to find ways and means to get things done. If you ask a professional he will go by the book. Suppose you ask him to go there and the door is closed? He will come back and say "I tried, the keys are not working." But the guy who is an entrepreneur will not accept this answer. He will say there will be some ways and means. He will find some window or find a way to fix the door, hmm?' he explained, chuckling. 'Failure is not an option, and, the word impossible doesn't go in his head. Next to impossible is only possible, no?' he added.

He points to a framed photograph of the late Indian prime minister Indira Gandhi and recalls how in 1974 he took her to Iran, where his family firm was then headquartered, when India was struggling with rising oil prices. 'At that time Iran started getting lot of money from the crude oil prices when it jumped to $34. What used to be 2.40 went to 11 then it went to 24,' he explained. When Mrs Gandhi complained at the impact of these increases on India, the Shah is reported to have urged her to sell more Indian goods to Iran. The Hindujas played a key role in the trade, and continue to do so today.

I asked him about K. K. Modi's potato story, and he said it was true. In 1973, not long after Indira Gandhi's army had inflicted a humiliating defeat on Pakistan's forces in the 1971 war which divided East and West Pakistan to create an independent Bangladesh, G. P. received word that the Shah needed their help to relieve an unfolding food crisis. Iran relies heavily on potatoes and onions but a scarcity had sent prices soaring. The short-term answer was to simply import them, but the country's otherwise booming economy, fuelled by rising global oil prices, had put its beleaguered ports under siege from ships carrying imports. Some were waiting up to three months to drop their cargoes.

'In Iran the Shah was most popular, very stable, everyone said it's the most stable country in the Middle East. And all the ports were congested because there was so much imports that there was a waiting time for two months and three months for the vessels to get unloaded.

'Three months! And they were paying heavy demurrages. And suddenly there was a shortage of a crop of potatoes and onions which used to be the most essential and staple food for the poor people. I remember the price of potato and onion, which used to be 5 rials per kilo, jumped up to 25 rials, it jumped up to about 100 rials and the voices and cries of the poor and middle-class people were [rising], okay, but what could the Shah do?'

He called the Hindujas because they had acquired a reputation for getting difficult things done and finding solutions where others scratched their heads. 'He invites the commerce minister, he invites his cabinet, he discusses. They said "we have a problem. We have no port where we can unload it." So the Shah told them: "Look, I know a family who are very [much] entrepreneurs" and he asked the commerce minister, Fereidoun Mahdavi, to ask the Hindujas to fill each and every town and city of Iran with potatoes and onions,' he said. When Mahdavi asked how the family would do it, the Shah told his cabinet: "Look, you don't get concerned about it, they'll do it. I know entrepreneurs can do everything".'

Mahdavi called G. P. and told him the Shah wanted the family to find a way to import enough onions and potatoes to bring their prices down from 100 rials to 5, money no object. G. P. called his older brother Srichand in Mumbai to ask how they might meet the challenge. 'He says I have a newspaper in front of me, there is flood of crops of potatoes and onions in Amritsar and Jalandhar and all the total crop is going wasted.' All they needed to do was buy the glut in Punjab, transport it 1,200 kilometres through Pakistan to Zahedan, just over its border in Iranian Baluchistan, and from there to local markets to bring the prices down. They simply needed the approval of Pakistan's Prime Minister Zulfikar Ali Bhutto and it could be done quickly.

No Indian trucks had been allowed on Pakistan's roads since Partition in 1947 and relations between the two countries were at a new low following the Bangladesh war. Pakistan did however have good relations with Iran, perhaps the Shah's ministers could help persuade Mr Bhutto to open his gates to India's potato trucks to help its friend in Tehran?

'The first call comes from the Foreign Minister of Iran [Abbas Ali] Khalatbari [who was later executed by the Ayatollah Khomeini regime following a show trial]. He said the Pakistani ambassador will call you, you tell him all you need and they will agree to facilitate. We started buying crops from the farmers in India and they were blessing the family, thanking God that there is someone to buy them,' he said, chuckling. They were loaded onto 1,400 trucks and driven to the India-Pakistan border at Wagah, a few kilometres from Amritsar, but just as they were about to make their historic journey, Pakistani intelligence officials brought them to a halt and said the drivers could be Indian spies. 'How can we allow them to get through the Pakistan border?' they asked.

After buying up enough potatoes and onions to feed Iran, the Hindujas were stranded with the consignment at the border in trucks without drivers and time running out. The Pakistanis agreed however to allow the convoy to pass through but only if they could find non-Indian nationals to drive them. Suddenly they had to find 1,400 non-Indian drivers from around the world, persuade them to come to India for a temporary job in poor conditions, arrange their visas and get them to the Wagah Border before the produce started to rot. They contacted international agencies, many of the drivers were flown in from Seoul in South Korea and in just under three weeks they had assembled an army of truckers to come to the Shah's rescue. 'We worked for twenty days, day and night, to make it a success, but that road was only open once, that's all...whatever drivers we found, we filled each and every town and village with potatoes and onions by road...it worked and in three weeks the prices went down to 5 rials and 6 rials and everything was normalized,' G. P. explained.

Just as K. K. Modi's sugar cane factory manager had promised to deliver milk for his family's wedding without knowing how, the Hindujas had given their word to the Shah that they would supply onions and potatoes and once given, it had to be honoured, whatever it took. 'If you ask professionals to do this they will say "sorry sir, we need six months". If I have to arrange a party, if I tell my office, you know what they will do? "Sir, we need four weeks, we need six weeks," whereas we manage it in forty-eight hours,' he said. What had it taken to fulfil his promise to the Shah? 'How did I do it? Now look, God gave me strength, ideas, thought, and it worked. Because I didn't want to accept the no and there was enthusiasm and zeal to see how we can help the common people and also help the [Iranian] government.'

Their success boosted their reputation further in Iran as resourceful people who could get difficult things done and the key was their 'jugaadism'—'something you do with extraordinary talent, you have to have an inspiration within you, enthusiasm, it is like a challenge. Thing comes in, how to manage it? [Who] is a master in crisis management? What is crisis management? Different ways of jugaadism,' he said. The practitioner of jugaadism works around the problem, doesn't take no for an answer and draws on willpower and lateral thinking to solve or bypass it. It is, he said, the antithesis of professionalism, practised by the 'box-headed'. 'They will only do what is written in the book,' he explained. 'The people in difficulty if they have this talent will manage anywhere. Otherwise people who don't have this talent, if there's no job, they get stuck,' he said.

Is he a jugaadi?

'No, what I do is entrepreneurship, but within the art of entrepreneurship jugaad is resorted to when needed.'

◆

Kunwer Sachdev's Porsche SUV is parked outside his gleaming

Su-Kam Power Systems headquarters in Gurgaon, the booming satellite city on the outskirts of Delhi. Today ,he is a multimillionaire many times over but he began his business career as a boy selling pens door to door on a pushbike. Like K. K. Modi and G. P. Hinduja he has relied on jugaad to make and increase his fortune. He is the self-styled 'Inverter Man of India', and his business empire has grown out of one of the country's greatest infrastructure failures— to build a reliable system to generate and supply electricity. In the face of this failure and the bleak prospect of it being fixed any time soon, millions of middle-class Indians simply found their own individual solutions in the power inverter: a machine which stores DC mains electricity on large batteries and automatically converts it to AC power during an 'outage' or 'load-shedding'. The rise to household necessity of the inverter holds within its tangle of wires the story of independent India and the resilience, individualism and resourcefulness of its people. It is an indictment of government failure, a monument to its people's fierce survival instinct and an insight into their expectations.

In the early 1970s in Britain, the depletion of coal stocks during a dispute between the Conservative government and the mine workers' union led to an official Three-Day Week to save electricity and regular power cuts. It caused a political crisis and brought down the government. The New York Blackouts in 1977 sparked protests, rioting and looting throughout the city and closed both John F. Kennedy and LaGuardia airports for eight hours. But when half the population of India was plunged into darkness in July 2012, protests were limited to a few sound bites on its twenty-four-hour news channels and a claim by the leader of its anti-corruption movement that it was part of a conspiracy to undermine his threatened but not enacted 'fast unto death'. The reality was that India was more familiar with power failure than uninterrupted supply—one-third of those living in rural areas had no electricity in any case and many of those who did have electricity had only intermittent 'bijli'. It did not become a political issue which united people in protest partly because so many, especially middle-class Indians, had no expectation that the government would solve the problem. Instead, they made their own private arrangements to work around it: those who could afford it relied on diesel-guzzling generators and inverters.

They are essentially a jugaad, a quick fix rather than a permanent system solution and the 'Inverter Man of India' came to dominate their manufacture by embracing jugaad from an early age.

Unlike K. K. Modi and the Hinduja brothers who were born into some wealth, Kunwer Sachdev was raised in Punjabi Bagh, West Delhi, by his lower middle-class family in some hardship. His father was a railway clerk who dreamed of being a businessman. He opened a grocery shop and launched a tailoring venture, but never found success. Kunwer wore hand-me-down shirts from his older brother, torn shoes were stitched and repaired to save money. 'Everything was scarce for us,' he said. One of his earliest deals was with other children in his neighbourhood who'd been sent by their parents to buy the daily bottle of morning milk. 'I had to get up in the morning and stand in the queue. Milk was finished if I was a little late. The moment I'm late I know I'm not going to get the bottle for my family and I'm going to get scolded by my father. So the moment I'm late I'll find a way out, you know, break that line so that I get the milk somehow, to push in, push in means I have to find a way... So I'm born and brought up where I have to look for solutions of my own problem, I have to solve my family's problem and my problem, I was looking for solutions. Now I look back and I realize that I had to look for so many solutions. In Britain or US a person does not have to develop their mind like that,' he said. At school, where he was often late, he found a low part of the boundary wall and made a makeshift step so he could climb over and go straight to the classroom without his teachers realizing he was tardy and sending him to be caned.

His business career began at fifteen, while still at school in the late 1960s, helping his brother sell pens door to door. He earned one rupee pocket money, which was enough for him to start dreaming big. He started thinking about manufacturing his own pens, making his own boxes, creating a brand and thought of the name 'Su-Kam'. The idea stayed with him when he studied mathematics and statistics at Delhi University's Hindu College, where he also sold his brother's pens to top up his income, and later when he got a job selling community cable television systems for apartment blocks.

In 1988, he struck out on his own, set up his business manufacturing cable television equipment without any technical training or knowledge from his father's shop in Punjabi Bagh. He learned fast, made amplifiers, directional couplers and modulators, the basic components of cable TV systems, and eventually satellite receivers and dishes. He made money but the frequent power cuts held him back. He had a generator at his factory and an inverter at home that regularly broke down. While watching the electrician during one of its many repairs, he decided he could make a better model. At that time inverters were bulky and 'having a jungle of wires'. They looked home-made and many of them were. It was a cottage industry based on copying machines made in Kolkata which then had India's worst power problems. His Su-Kam inverter would be sleeker, cheaper and longer-lasting. He asked a friend in Canada to bring him an inverter used to power the lights and kitchen appliances in caravans and campers based on a different technology known as MOSFET (metal oxide semiconductor field-effect transistor) and began adapting it to work in Indian homes. In the caravans the inverter stored electricity generated by the dynamo as it rolled along the highways, but to work in static homes it needed its own charging device. He began developing his own jugaad charger based on 'hit and try method' without understanding the concept behind it and got a 'big failure'. It kept short-circuiting. He gave a prototype to a friend to use in his home and tweaked it every time it failed, and eventually, after a year had a different inverter which worked. It was a quarter of the size of rival models, it used one battery instead of two, which made it cheaper, and it looked sleeker—it didn't have the 'jungle of wires'.

He started manufacturing them in his factory, selling them to his cable television clients and advertising them in newspapers. Today Su-Kam is one of the world's largest inverter and power electronics firms with a turnover of more than ₹850 crore. It is expanding into solar power systems to connect the poor in remote villages and developing new inverter systems in the safety-obsessed West. In Britain, most office stairs have inverter systems to run the emergency lights in case of fire or mains power failure.

He attributes his drive to become successful to the hardship and scarcity he grew up with and the knowledge that no government or welfare agency would solve his family's problems for them. 'In India there are a lot of challenges for the people, everyday challenges, and there is no one to solve for them. In other countries there is a government that takes care of the basics, people don't have to make any effort, but in India you have no choice other than to fend for yourself. So people do look for solutions and that becomes jugaad. I have a problem, no one is going to give me the answer for that problem, one way is I leave it, one way is I do it,' he explained.

Why did people in India tolerate the power cuts rather than put pressure on political leaders to solve the problem at its root? 'People in India are not aware that if you demand something it can be done. And the government is not in a position where if you demand they can fulfil. There is a gap between the expectations and the work done. In India if you buy something, some product, and you demand services and people don't fulfil it, you are used to it. How many people can you fight?' he explained.

India has one of the world's wealthiest elites, millionaires and billionaires who holiday in London, New York, Paris. Can they really not know how things could be, what good service might look like? 'But they come back and have to get used to it, even you have got used to it. If there is no electricity coming to your house, do you go and write an article and we'll come and listen?' he asked.

He is right. We 'adjusted', lowered our expectations and carefully maintained our inverter in the knowledge that the power supply wouldn't improve any time soon. We relied instead on our own personal solution and left the system to others to worry about.

My crorepatis have certainly never fretted over it. To them, every gap in delivery, every failing is an opportunity, a challenge to their sense of invincibility, their absolute belief that they will find a solution. Success in India, as K. K. Modi said, is achieved in spite of corruption, bad roads and all the other problems. And as G. P. Hinduja says 'Next to impossible is only possible, no?'

These tycoons are at one with my rough swadeshi inventors on this. Cigarettes, potatoes, inverters, cheap sanitary towels, fruit pulping machines and ice-based coolers. Their uplifting optimism and can-do certitude is India's USP and its soft power in the world. It's all possible, 100 per cent.

CHAPTER 4

'FOR MOST INDIANS 70 PER CENT IS GOOD ENOUGH'

The 'next to impossible is only possible' optimism shared by my frugal and crorepati jugaadis reminded me of 'The Sculptor', a much-loved television commercial shown in Britain before we moved to India in 2005. A young driver, sweating the summer heat in a small dust-blown town, probably in Rajasthan, is looking across its main square to his tatty, white Ambassador car. Its headlamps are missing; prayer beads dangle from the mirror; a blurry plastic religious icon is glued to the dashboard.

Possessed, he marches through the camel-cart traffic, jumps into the car, stamps the pedal to the metal and crashes into the wall in front. He reverses fast to smash its dicky into the one behind and then leads an elephant to sit on its bonnet and squash it into a sleeker shape. Flakes of paint fly as he bashes it with hammers and burns a crackling welding torch through the night. In the morning light he looks up from a magazine spread of the sharp new Peugeot 206 of his dreams to his battered, rough approximation and wobbles his head in deep satisfaction. In his pimped and dented ride he is transformed from small-town chotu to Rajasthani road god, and the ad closes with him cruising the streets, jaw jutting to bhangra beats and checking out sidewalk beauties who turn their heads in desire. Next to impossible is only possible, isn't it?

It is a work of comic genius which hints that its award-winning director, Giovanni Porro, understood the importance of jugaad in Indian life long before its new gurus made it a management philosophy and many years ahead of me. Our young sculptor isn't daunted by scarcity or poverty, and he sets out to make what he can't buy with the materials he has to hand—Ambassador car, elephant, thick city walls, sledgehammer. The result is no showroom model but it's good enough for him, his crew and the babes of his town.

It chimed with K. K. Modi's definition of jugaad as a fix which achieves an objective even though it may not necessarily be the best solution. It rang a lot of bells. The Snowbreeze, my inspiring blue trashcan cooler, was a work in progress, a workshop prototype in search of a designer—it kind of worked but made a mess of the front yard and didn't quite cool enough. Dharamveer Kamboj's fruit processing machine spun a new life of comfort and status for his family, but it sprays a lot of pulp onto the floor. Arunachalam Muruganantham's sanitary towels for poor women are not quite the liberation their inventor had wished for them. A survey in villages near Hubli, Karnataka, found complaints that they didn't stick or stay in place—a serious issue for those working in the fields. Younger women complained that they didn't have wings and were too bulky for comfort. In short, their inventions were uplifting, but rough. They were almost good enough, almost fit for purpose, but looked unfinished—like the ambitious project of a promising high school student—and shoddiness seemed to be built-in.

It was there too in my own Ambassador, previously owned by the Church of North India and every bit the civil service babu's carriage—white windscreen sun visor, yellow-film headlamps, steering column handbrake and puce velour seats. I'd paid ₹90,000 for it and it was, initially, a key ingredient in living out our Indian dream. It was, in some ways, a jugaad purchase. I needed a cheap car which could fit all five of us—me, my tall wife, three young children and driver to negotiate the special perils of Indian roads. The front bucket seats were ripped out and replaced with a retro bench to fit three— me on the left, driver on the right and our then eight-year-old in the middle where his right leg was bruised with every change into second gear. The dicky door, with its chrome turnkey handle, didn't quite fit or shut with a smooth clunk, it had to be jiggled in. I had the engine overhauled, the seats reupholstered in fawn leatherette, and a small Scottish saltire flag and pole fitted on the passenger side wing for fun. Police officers in Haryana and Himachal Pradesh would stand to attention and salute, just in case, as we passed by.

It was a cobbled together, temporary solution using locally-available materials, but the joy I felt every time I saw its friendly face soon gave way to irritation. It kept breaking down and although it was often repaired by a roadside mechanic who would miraculously appear whenever I stopped to open the hood, it was increasingly in the workshop for ever more expensive work. According to the workshop manager, I'd bought a faulty model which was controlled by a defective cable no longer in stock. They were occasionally available in the motor parts bazaars of Old Delhi and if I found some I should buy the lot for all the future repairs it will undoubtedly need, he advised. Cuteness has its limits and the love I felt for my Amby began to wane as the complaints from my family reached a crescendo. My teenage children were growing ever taller—I was now the chotu in our family—and the Ambassador's limited leg room was becoming a cause of daily squabbles.

For the first and only time in my life, I decided to buy a new car and to let the children choose it so they had no cause for later complaint. Budget restricted the choice to Mahindra's 'rufty-tufty' Scorpio SUV or its new and cheaper Xylo MUV (multi-utility vehicle)—which came with more bells and whistles and a television ad which showed how its seats all reclined to turn the car into a king-sized bed. The leggy Nelsons got their way and chotu wrote the cheque. Though grumpy over the outlay (any outlay), I loved it, but while looking for something in the rear seat a few weeks later, I noticed a gap between a plastic covering panel over the rear passenger side wheel arch. On closer inspection, the overlapping panel had a shard missing which looked like it had been chipped in production or delivery. When I asked about it at the dealer's workshop, the manager said all Xylos came like that. 'You mean it's a design feature?' I asked in disbelief. 'Yes, sir,' he replied as he beckoned me to the car lot at the back to look at other new Xylos. I climbed into the back and, sure enough, the wheel arch had the same sheared panel.

Mahindra is one of India's leading companies but it seemed even the country's best could, occasionally, be rough around the edges. My pernickety disappointment at finding flaws in my perfect new car prompted a question. If the very best sometimes settled for just good enough over excellence, what hope was there that India would become the world leader in every area of endeavour its ambitious people desperately want it to be?

Excellence is an ugly word but I started to crave it in India. Its economy was then growing at more than 8 per cent, second only to China among major economies, and the belief that India would overtake it was widely held. But, with the occasional exception of its cricket team and heritage architecture, it was difficult to find contemporary things which could, fairly, be described as excellent. I kept finding the word on the tip of my tongue whenever I was offered something barely good enough or hugely disappointing—an expensive hotel brunch rounded off with Delhi Belly, or the often dirty toilets which belied the five stars of many seemingly grand hotels; plumbing repairs which lasted for just days; painters who smudged all the edges, spilled paint and plaster on the floor and regarded it as my job to clean up; electricians who left dangerous live cables poking out from a wall or connected wires to the wrong switches and insisted it was fine. By 2010, India felt like home, our three children had almost grown up here, and I wanted it to be the best it could be. The cuteness I loved as a passing correspondent irritated me as a long-term resident and I yearned for it to catch up fast and meet the needs people were increasingly crying out for: reliable electricity and sufficient water, safe and modern public transport, good roads and hospitals.

There were reasons to be optimistic. The Commonwealth Games in Delhi later that year was a catalyst for change and large infrastructure projects had turned the city upside down in the drive to transform it in time for the world to see it with new eyes. A new airport terminal was underway, the city's rusty and battered Blueline buses, regularly in the news for mowing down pedestrians, were being replaced by a smart new fleet. New roads were under construction and the tentacles of the world's cheapest Metro system were spreading fast above and below them.

It finally reached our South Delhi neighbourhood in September, a few weeks before the games opening ceremony, and I felt excited about the new world of possibility it opened up. The station was a few hundred metres from our doorstep and its gleaming metallic Bombardier trains could have you in the heart of Old Delhi's bazaars in less than half an hour. Suddenly the world's finest kebabs were just a short hop away. It was a significant milestone on Delhi's road to modernity and cause for optimism. The first phase had been completed three years ahead of schedule by Indian engineering firms, its gleaming steel trains were frequent, and its creator, the humble veteran railway chief, E. Sreedharan, had delivered it without a murmur of corruption: He donated his salary to charity, preferring to survive on his Indian Railways pension, lived an ascetic life and yoga appeared to be his only vice. His creation looked a lot like excellence by any standards and certainly compared favourably with the London Underground and New York Metro.

I was at the ticket counter within hours of our station's opening, drooling at the prospect of chicken korma and desperate to see India's best at work. As I walked down the steps, I noticed jagged holes had been hammered through its marble walls for the cables and pipes its designers had overlooked. There were gaps between wonky panels on the ceiling, paan stains already striped the skirtings. It looked like a long snag list which would be made good in time, but in fact the list got longer as the months and years passed. When I arrived at Chawri Bazar, you could see the same snags writ larger—impossibly tangled and dangerously dipping overhead cables, rickshaw gridlock in flooded galis, fine nineteenth-century haveli town houses defaced by ad hoc extensions, verandas annexed in glass as extra rooms, and in the damp monsoon air the pungent, omnipresent scent of urine.

Although I was disappointed by the Delhi Metro's shortcomings, my quest to find world-class India continued, and in October the following year, siren hope called out again with a breathless government announcement that it was about to unveil a technological breakthrough which could transform the lives of the world's poorest. The 'world's cheapest computer' had gained a reputation among foreign correspondents as the story that cried wolf. In 2009, Indian officials had unveiled the '$10 laptop' which turned out to be neither a laptop nor available for $10 but a storage device which could serve as a component in a laptop which might cost $60. It was denounced in the *Times of India* as a 'damp squib'.

The following year officials promised a $35 laptop that aroused some scepticism—after all, the pioneers at the celebrated One Laptop Per Child campaign (founded by Nicholas Negroponte at MIT's lab) were struggling to make one for $100. But when the Ministry of Human Resources sent out invitations to a grand launch event with school children from all around India, I couldn't help but share the excitement. India, after all, has yielded some of the world's smartest information technologists and many of them are now in charge of some of the biggest firms in Silicon Valley: one in three of the tech giant Apple's engineers are Indian while Microsoft is now run by Satya Nadella who was born in Hyderabad and went on to study at Karnataka's Manipal Institute of Technology and Madurai-born Sundar Pichai is the CEO of Google after its reorganization in 2015.

Behind the ceremonial curtain was the gadget the world was waiting for: Aakash, not a $10 laptop, but a tablet and at $35 the world's cheapest computer, or, as the ministry officials called it, Low Cost Access-cum-Computing Device (LCAD). It would take poor and remote students into college lecture theatres from the comfort of their own houses by offering video-based courses online. The minister who had championed the project, Kapil Sibal, an accomplished lawyer, took the stage and set the scene for what he described as a historical event. 'What can I say? There will be some moments in history which will be milestones recognized by future generations. This is one such moment. Today we see the beginning of a dream realized, a dream in which every student in every corner of this country will have access to technology which defines the twenty-first century. Today we reach for the sky and achieve what others said was impossible. Today we demonstrate to the world we will not falter in our resolve to secure the future for our children,' he said.

The Aakash was the beginning of a technological revolution for poor Indian children and families around the world: 'This is not just for us but for all of you who are disempowered, all of you who have no access, those who are marginalized, who live on the fringes of society, let us, the world together, the tech providers of the world, social activists of the world, the stakeholders, the children of the global community, let them partner with us so we can provide to the world a device which costs less than $10!' he said with a flourish.

At that moment, the government's greatest challenge was in persuading families to enrol and keep their children at school. Just over half of secondary age children attended classes according to UNICEF figures collected between 2008 and 2012. The 40 to 50 per cent of children not attending were not guaranteed access to chalk or pencils, let alone a Low Cost Access-cum-Computing Device. It was hard not to admire the government's ability to gaze, undaunted, beyond the grim reality of primary and secondary education in India to a sky without limits or the minister's fighting talk.

The device's creator, Canadian–Indian Suneet Singh Tuli, followed the minister's lead. 'A lot of things were said about this project, [that it was] simply impossible. It was not just that it was impossible, others said that Indians can't do it. It can't be done by Indians or in India. The worst was when people said they wish it would never happen. We hope our role is to make this vision a reality. Allow me to introduce the world's lowest cost computing Internet device by Datawind,' he said, unveiling the Aakash.

His presentational flair, his black suit and matching turban, gave him the air of a Sikh Steve Jobs and he agreed his Aakash tablet was the 'anti-iPad', a device for the poorest rather than a symbol of exclusive wealth and Western domination. My newspaper was excited at the idea of a £22 'iPad' and asked if I could file my story on the device as a world first. Suneet Singh Tuli's army of helpers set up the device for me in a media room and I got to work. Its touchscreen was not hard or glassy like an iPad but spongy which made it slow for typing, but I managed to finish my story on what was, at that point, an uplifting tale.

Carefully, I copied the text so I could paste it into an email to file to London and asked one of the staff about the Wi-Fi connection. As we tried to figure it out, my text simply disappeared and couldn't be retrieved. Helpers of ascending seniority intervened to recover a good story breaking bad, but no one could find the missing copy. There was no 'undo' function, the 'copy' command appeared to be dysfunctional and the file had vanished without trace. I approached Suneet Singh Tuli in the hope that he would know what to do, but he didn't and the text was permanently lost. The story was rewritten later with an unhappier ending and what was to be an Indian triumph was another public relations disaster.

The sight of the late Steve Jobs in his trademark black polo neck unveiling Apple's latest revolutionary gadget was a regular yardstick of consumer progress throughout the nineties and noughties. The pre-launch speculation and the excitement it generated were fuelled by an expectation of excellence. And while his products had glitches (which were addressed by later updates) at their launch events, they worked and received a worldwide wow. The Aakash, however, had made India's government look silly. It may have been on to something, but it wasn't ready for launch. Why had the government unveiled it before basic glitches had been worked out? Given that the minister wanted to use the occasion to inspire the world, why had its creators not insisted upon high quality performance before opening themselves to ridicule?

Its failure seemed to be of a piece. The Aakash looked like a poor man's iPad in the same way 'The Sculptor's' battered and elephant-squashed Ambassador looked like a home-made Peugeot 206. Instead of sealing India's reputation as a technology pioneer, it highlighted its roughness, a careless 'just good enough' approach and a readiness to celebrate the substandard. It raised a bigger question too. India had at various times throughout several millennia led the world in science and technology. There was in earlier times a high regard for academic rigour, a culture of excellence. Why was it proving so hard to find in modern India?

I put my question to Professor Gupta of the Honey Bee Network, champion of India's frugal innovators, and his answer brought a moment of revelation. Like many in India, he too was frustrated by the roughness and ugliness of its products, he said.

'I've seen bad joints on the tiles in hotel bathrooms and washbasins, where you see the failure. If you live in India you find that. I notice that and I don't like it. When you fit a unit to the wall, there should be no dust settling between it and the wall. Attention to detail, finessing and aesthetics where something has to be beautiful is missing,' he said. Subrahmanyan Chandrasekhar, the Nobel Prize-winning Indian astrophysicist, had written about how the products of good science must be beautiful, he said, but in India there is 'a disconnect with this instinct and peculiarity in our genes'. He cited the example of roadside mechanics who make espresso coffee machines by attaching a pipe to pressure cookers—effective and cheap, but ugly. 'He may do a good job but not finish it because he doesn't have the tools,' he said. On the other hand, the West has made a fetish of accuracy and excellence, which is exclusive and sometimes self-destructive, he added. I, he said, had noticed the small fault in my Xylo car because I'd been raised and trained in that culture. 'You cannot overlook Indian ruggedness,' he explained, 'but I do believe that accuracy and affordability can be traded off.'

The costliness of high quality Western medicines was a case in point, he said. 'If you have a drug which cures 99.9 per cent of the time at $100 per tablet, and another at 80 per cent but costs $1, no side effects, no [Western] drug company would touch that $1 drug because it is only 80 per cent. The majority of the people of our country will have a solution at 70 per cent. Nature will take care of the rest, why do I have to solve everything? Solutions are affordable because they meet the trade-off. The main Western ideal makes a fetish of accuracy, disregarding the poor people of the world [for whom] 80 per cent is a great advance. Why should we reject 80 per cent?' In India, home to one-third of the world's poor living on less than $1.90 per day, the minute error margins of Western science are unaffordable but there's plenty of cheap utility for them in less accurate but adequately effective products and services.

'So that's the lesson of frugal innovation. We don't try to solve to 95 per cent accuracy, but look at 75 per cent, 80 per cent and go ahead and work out a solution. There are lessons to be learned from India about new ways of thinking which have helped society survive,' he said.

It was an epiphany, a facepalm moment and there were echoes of Fritz Schumacher's *Small is Beautiful* in his conclusion. Mr Lal's inspiring Snowbreeze certainly cooled at around the 70 per cent mark, Arunachalam Muruganantham's sanitary pads were fairly absorbent if uncomfortable and 'The Sculptor's' battered, home-made 'Peugeot' did, at least in rough outline, resemble the picture.

According to Professor Gupta, this is part of an 'Indian heuristic' which should be discussed and celebrated. 'They have a way of tweaking a problem and leave the user to optimize it or nature to solve,' he said. Professor Gupta had raised an important point. The 'trial and error'—or 'hit and trial' as my inverter tycoon calls it—approach is a universal phenomenon on which India has no monopoly. The jugaad exploration and innovation it leads to has well-loved versions around the world. In Britain, the term 'Heath Robinson' conjures images of convoluted lever and pulley machines to carry out simple functions, like the 'well-thought out and nearly successful experiment by early railway pioneer' featuring a top-hatted Victorian gentleman riding a steam-powered, wooden-wheeled and propeller-driven 'train' with a candle lamp for night use. Many of his drawings became children's classics in the Professor Branestawm books. More recently the same 'hit and trial' method of innovation was celebrated in the Oscar-winning Wallace and Gromit cartoon films: Wallace, the northern England shed-based inventor has a machine which tips him out of bed into his clothes and down a chute onto a kitchen chair where a mechanical arm slaps a piece of buttered toast down in front of him. He invents remote-control 'techno trousers' to walk his silent, eternally sceptical, dog Gromit as 'a valuable addition to our modern lifestyle'.

We laugh because we all know a Wallace-type tinkerer or handyman, we have all seen Heath Robinson-style contraptions. They stand on one of the great fault lines in our understanding of how people think and why they make the decisions they do: Is man a rational optimizer striving for perfection or a 'satisficer' who will pick the first option seen as good enough? Herbert Simon, the celebrated American social scientist, galvanized the debate in the 1950s when he coined the term 'bounded rationality' to argue that because people did not have perfect knowledge or infinite time to explore all the alternatives, they used imperfect heuristics to make decisions. Others in his wake, like the German Gerd Gigerenzer, suggested decisions are made using an 'adaptive toolbox', a range of sub-optimal methodologies for selecting courses of action or choices. We follow the judgements of others to save time, we favour the familiar. We don't spend a lifetime searching for the perfect, ultimate mate or house, but choose one which seems good enough or the best available at that moment. We fall in love, he suggested, as a 'stopping mechanism' against infinite search. William C. Wimsatt, professor emeritus of philosophy at the University of Chicago compared man's decision-making style to a 'backwoods mechanic and used-parts dealer'—a fair description of our frugal jugaadi innovators and a reflection of Professor Gupta's 'Indian heuristic'.

Suneet Singh Tuli's Aakash should be seen in that context and certainly not as a failure—it will eventually be regarded as a great success, Professor Gupta suggested. 'There are two million orders for Aakash. I think it will be successful. Aakash is 80 per cent and good enough at one-tenth of the price. They should have urban and rural versions. It could revolutionize the teaching of biology and geography,' he said. Not for the first time, Professor Gupta left me feeling a little ashamed of my growing cynicism. Perhaps, in my rush to judgement and to meet a deadline, I'd been harsh. I needed to give Mr Tuli a fairer hearing.

Suneet Singh Tuli told me that since he and his brother Raja founded Datawind in 2001, they had been developing software and devices to lure India's legion of mobile phone users onto the Internet. India is the fastest growing mobile phone market in the world and its growth has been driven by $10 Chinese handsets that have made them affordable to poor farm labourers and cycle rickshawwalas alike. By 2013, India's 1.2 billion population had almost 900 million mobile phone connections despite being home to 400 million of the world's poorest people living on less than $1.25 per day. The mobile phone had reached the very bottom of the pyramid—the 2011 Census confirmed that while only 46.9 per cent of Indian homes had a toilet, 63.2 per cent had a telephone. Many of the poorest had seen the benefits of connectivity. Small farmers received vital weather forecasts as text messages, while handcart sabziwalas selling fruits and vegetables on the move were able to take advance orders. The Tulis had been developing browsers which could load web pages on cheap handsets and slow 2G networks in a few seconds to open the Internet to India's poorest.

They had also been lobbying the government to support their vision since 2003 but made no progress until 2009 when Nicholas Negroponte's Miami-based One Laptop Per Child group captured the world's imagination with its drive for a $100 device. India had declined to support the project which it regarded as a challenge to its USP: Tata, its largest company, had just launched the Nano, the 'One Lakh Car', the world's cheapest family vehicle; *Chandrayaan*, the lowest cost lunar space mission was underway. The world's cheapest computer device was India's to build and the government was not about to cede the turf to rich encroachers from Miami. Their attitude towards One Laptop Per Child was 'if you can do it, we can do it better and cheaper and no-one can do it as cheap as we can,' Suneet Singh Tuli explained. 'Now politicians who rejected One Laptop Per Child were looking for ways to prove themselves right.' Ministers' attempts to persuade India's largest IT players to develop a credible low-cost device had failed. Their '500 rupee laptop' Sakshat (before your eyes) was exposed as a smoke and mirrors illusion and finally they turned to Suneet Singh Tuli in whom they found a kindred spirit.

As children he and his brother emigrated from Punjab to Canada where they received a 'world class education' their playmates in Chandigarh had been denied. They grew up conscious of their own good fortune and concerned for those they'd left behind. Their motivation, however, was commercial rather than philanthropic. Suneet Singh Tuli is a true champion of cheap, a jugaad innovator who believes customers will always choose a cheaper option over higher quality if it meets enough of their basic requirements.

He and his team studied the growth of computer use in the United States to predict a price tipping point for India—how cheap would a tablet computer need to be to become affordable to the masses? They found that in the US it had been when the price of a computer dropped below $1,000, which was then one week's average American wage. In India, in 2009, that figure was around $50 (₹2,350 at the prevailing exchange rates)—still not within the reach of its poorest but close enough to the bottom of the pyramid for take off. The Aakash tablet—sold commercially as UbiSlate—offered a 366 MHz processor, 2 GB of RAM storage device which ran on the Android operating system for ₹2,500, and Suneet Singh Tuli believed its value for money would give India its own IT tipping point. His thinking is strongly influenced by Clayton M.

Christensen, the Harvard Business School professor and author of *The Innovator's Dilemma* which explains how successful companies making advanced, high-end products are often toppled by new rivals offering lower-quality, poor-performing cheaper versions.

Suneet Singh Tuli believes his Aakash poses the same threat. His first Aakash may have had only 2 GB of memory, a spongy screen and unresolved glitches in its Android operating system, but it worked at a certain level and, at ₹2,500, it was a bargain—almost ₹25,000 cheaper than a Samsung Galaxy, ₹28,000 less than the iPad 2 at the time of its launch, and more importantly, affordable to millions of Indians for whom any tablet computer was a distant dream. 'Affordability truly does matter in the Indian market, [there's a] sort of a fine balance between what's good enough and how affordable it needs to be. When I do presentations around frugal innovation I talk about the "disruption of the good enough"; inexpensive and good enough technology consistently beats expensive and very good technology,' he explained. 'When you look at breaking those price barriers, it is focusing on trying to achieve what is good enough, what the consumer will accept and continuing to iterate that onwards. And over time the product will meet the expectations of even the high-end user,' he added.

Since its launch, the Aakash has been improved, launched commercially, and is now a serious challenger to Apple and Samsung in India, with more than a million devices sold, he said.

In the three years since its launch it has evolved to the point where Tuli believes it is technologically comparable with its expensive Western rivals. His first Aakash had a 366 MHz processor compared to the first iPad's faster, 1 GHz processor speed. Both had 256 MB of RAM storage. Aakash 2, however, matched the early iPad's Cortex 1 GHz processor and increased its RAM storage to 512 MB. 'Even though it was a few years after the first iPad, the question I would ask is "is it not good enough at one-tenth of the price?" [The] sort of $40 that we came down to, having the same horsepower as the original iPad, is that not good enough for what we're trying to do for our target markets?' he said. His device's next model, the Aakash 4, will match the current iPad model for processing speed and memory storage, he claimed. The cheap, lower quality product does not outperform its expensive superior but it improves to the point where even high-end consumers are willing to accept its lower grade features because it is cheaper. He cites the example of Betamax video which was widely regarded as technically superior to VHS, but lost the battle because its rival was cheaper and had enough storage to record feature films. Sales of Android-based smartphones have overtaken those of higher spec iPhones because customers get more for less. Despite the superior quality of digital camera photographs, most people make do with the poorer quality pictures taken with their mobile phones—it saves the cost of a camera, it's more convenient than carrying two gadgets and the photos are good enough. India's failure, to date, to produce the kind of obsessive excellence Steve Jobs personified at Apple is a feature of scale, he suggests.

'To meet the requirements of the masses, affordability becomes very important—even more important than excellence,' he said.

The rise of Walmart's cheap, bazaar-style stores in the United States and its eclipse of the higher quality Sears chain is another case in point. Few believed customers would prefer the upstart's tacky Chinese-made products to the well-made wares on offer at its upscale rival. Its victory on the way to global domination showed that 'even in the US market, affordability and good enough matters a lot more than the pursuit of excellence'.

Was there not something to be said for a little more excellence, when the lack of it had led to his Aakash launch being overshadowed by its faults and widely ridiculed? A simple autosave function and better word processing software would have saved my copy on its launch date and transformed a bad story into an effusive one. He had seen my pain and frustration at the launch of Aakash, he said, and he had addressed it shortly after by including Kingsoft Office Suite, a free Chinese word processing application which included an autosave function. The fault, he said, had been in the Android operating system but he and his brother had not been too downhearted about it. It was simply one of the never-ending series of glitches tech innovators spend their lives working out, and Steve Jobs was no different, he said. The early iPhone models had serious voice and antenna faults which were resolved after widespread complaints. Apple's Newton Personal Digital Assistant (PDA), a proto-iPad, was famously scrapped after errors in its predictive text software, its killer feature, were lampooned in the Doonesbury comic strip for transcribing the words 'catching on' as 'egg freckles'. For Tuli, each flaw and setback is simply another technology challenge and the precursor of the next iteration. The difference, he said, is in the price. In 1993, the flawed Newton MessagePad went on sale for $699—$664 more than the first Aakash in 2011. The faults that proved intolerable in such an expensive gadget are an acceptable trade-off in one so cheap, he argued. 'If you buy a pack of matchsticks and the first one doesn't work, you don't go for a refund, you say "okay let me try the second matchstick." Because at a certain price point you're prepared to go through that inconvenience. Now, what is that fine balance of the level of inconvenience you may be willing to go through?' he asked. It is a penetrating question and while the answers could never fully explain India's many daunting problems, they certainly litter its social, political and economic landscape.

CHAPTER 5

BAD JUGAAD

Anand Mahindra is one of India's most revered businessmen, a leading captain of industry and the chairman of one of its most progressive companies. The Mahindra Group has stakes in the automobile industry, farming equipment, IT, financial services, clean energy, urban lifestyle and defence.

I met him via Twitter after the air conditioner in my new Mahindra Xylo stopped working in its first year, just a few days before we were about to set off on our annual sixteen-hour drive from Delhi up to the Kullu Valley in the Himalayan foothills to escape the summer heat. The workshop manager said they were too busy to repair it in time and our holiday seemed doomed. Without air conditioning, the gruelling journey up the Grand Trunk Road in forty-degree temperatures would be unbearable, and I took to Twitter to voice my frustration.

Within minutes Anand Mahindra's office tracked me down and one of his assistants assured me the problem would be fixed. The workshop would stay open all night if necessary. He was as good as his word and we were soon on our way. Shortly after our 5 a.m. start along the Grand Trunk Road to the hills, a Mahindra workshop manager in Chandigarh, a few hours down the track, called to say he and his staff were on stand-by. Any problems, they would guide us in and put it right. After Chandigarh, another call, this time from the manager of Mahindra's Mandi workshop, higher up in the foothills, with the same message. We were being watched and taken care of every mile of our summer road trip.

It would, of course, have been better if the Delhi workshop had responded when asked, and a more edifying story if I hadn't used my profile as a foreign correspondent to demand it. But the company's commitment to excellence, at least at the highest level, couldn't be doubted. The boss was on it and seventeen hours later we were looking out over the apple orchards from a Kath-kuni stone and pine cottage at the moonlit peaks and ridges of the high Himalaya, bathing in the soft mountain breeze.

Was 70 per cent good enough for him? Had jugaad quick-fixes played a key role in Mahindra's rise?

When I called him for an interview for this book, he was fierce. If it was another paean to jugaad as the elixir of Indian enterprise, then no, he was not interested at all, thank you. In fact, jugaad was a mortal threat to India's development, he said, and he would only help if my book reflected that. I'd been in India for seven years at this point, and some, perhaps many, of its jugaad ways had rubbed off on me. I hedged. It would look at the good and bad but I agreed it was probably not the best way forward.

En route to meeting him in Mumbai, I stopped off at his Mahindra Research Valley, two hours' drive from Chennai, to check whether Anand Mahindra protested too much and if his own company operations really reflected his passionate rejection of jugaad. The 125-acre site is a ₹650 crore state-of-the-art R & D hub set within its own 'World City', a special economic zone (SEZ). The area has a Holiday Inn, offices and factories for some of India's leading hi-tech companies like Wipro and Infosys along with Western car giants Renault and BMW. It looks like an architect's model—quiet roads with street furniture, manicured lawns, neat pavement sidewalks and functioning traffic lights—India as seen in aspirational television ads but rarely on the ground. Its main building, designed by the celebrated Indian architect, the late Charles Correa, more closely resembles an international airport than a car factory and Anand Mahindra's staff lost no time in demonstrating that here, things are done differently.

After passing through one of the most rigorous security checks I have experienced—no cameras, recording devices—we stop in the vast lobby to take in the firm's 'innovation wall' where staff are reminded, and inspired, by the great thinkers, scientists and inventors of Indian history. There is Srinivasa Ramanujan, regarded as one of twentieth century's greatest natural mathematics geniuses. A few portraits along is Sir Chandrasekhara Venkata Raman, the Nobel Prize winning scientist who discovered how light scatters when it passes through transparent materials.

The moustachioed Victorian visage of Sir Jagadish Chandra Bose, the plant physiologist, physicist and father of modern wireless communications, stared out from the montage, alongside Aryabhata, the Vedic mathematician. There were portraits of Homi Bhabha, the father of India's nuclear energy programme, Satyendra Nath Bose, the pioneering physicist and correspondent of Einstein, and more recently, Sabeer Bhatia, the founder of Hotmail.

Dr Aravind Bharadwaj, Mahindra's vice president for technology, motioned me on, explaining that the wall highlights the company's philosophy—to inspire all of its employees to think creatively and find new solutions and products by reminding them of other Indians who have achieved greatness in their fields. A gap between portraits is an invitation to their staff to rise up and join them. As we moved on, through the landscaped central courtyard garden, Dr Bharadwaj asked if I knew that India has the highest number of exporters outside of Japan who are 'Deming Certified'—those who have met the American management guru's 'total quality' business systems. 'I believe strongly that Indian engineering prowess is there, there is no reason why we can't do it,' he said. To encourage their design engineers to do just that, Charles Correa's building has a landscaped garden at its heart and each office overlooks its trees and pond. It is, Dr Bharadwaj explains, designed to encourage them to mingle, collaborate and keep sustainability front of mind.

There are teleconferencing suites so they can also talk to their research colleagues at the company's technical centres in Detroit and

South Korea. Each of their collaborations begins with an analysis of all performance data from their previous product to make sure all weaknesses and errors are addressed and lessons learned incorporated into the next model.

Simulators that can replicate any road surface and weather condition are connected to every working part to measure its performance. 'All faults are simulated and corrected,' Dr Bharadwaj explained. There are laboratories refining the company's stop-start mechanisms that quietly turn the engine off at traffic lights and on again to reduce fuel consumption while idling. Mahindra has developed its own indigenous systems and was the first to introduce them in India. 'You don't feel it, it stops the moment you put your foot on the clutch and starts again before you touch the gear,' he said, proudly. At the design stage the system is tested through 300,000 cycles of stopping and starting. His engineers are now developing the next generation of lower cost hybrid electric–diesel cars to make them affordable in India. 'We've cracked it but it's about sustainability and price point,' he said. The company's acquisition of Reva electric cars has accelerated this work and yielded thirty-five of Mahindra Research Valley's 300 patents filed in the last three years. Much of its thinking focuses on the unique nature of Indian roads and the way the country's drivers ply them. They drive in extreme temperatures, on potholed roads and usually very close together. We passed by the rapid prototyping lab where a newly designed engine part can be made in plastic from the drawing on the same day for fast experimentation. There were labs where rubber parts are exposed to ozone, plastic components to all temperatures to establish their expected life span and test alternative materials.

The plant and its staff are real time testimony to Anand Mahindra's loathing of the jugaad he believes holds India back and that it needs to quickly move on from. But even here, among the most highly educated and trained engineers working with state of the art technology and in rigorous quality management systems, the phenomenon has not yet been entirely purged.

In one section of the laboratory, where components were being tested in temperature-controlled units, one keen young researcher opened the door, mid-test cycle, for me to get a closer look inside. He was being deferential, trying to please the guest, but it was a clear breach of the laboratory rules and had compromised the test. His error was quickly spotted by his manager, who scolded him: 'If it can't be opened, don't open it!' he said. It was a tiny glitch in what had been an impressive showcasing of Mahindra's world-class work in developing new and lower cost technologies. But it also highlighted the scale of the task in changing a flexible work culture where accommodations can always be made and rules bent, to one where the uncompromising discipline of scientific management must be rigidly maintained.

Tackling that accommodating approach requires eternal vigilance, Dr Bharadwaj explained later. 'First time right, every time right. Do not feel afraid, if something is wrong we have to put our hands up and say this is the way it should be done, to get into people's mindset and psyche. We're trying to put in that discipline and rigour and that comes from the very top.'

Anand Mahindra's office in Mumbai's Apollo Bunder, tucked in a lane behind the landmark Taj Mahal Palace Hotel and the Gateway of India, looks like the library of a London gentleman's club and the chairman exudes the assurance of a senior member in high standing. He is immaculately groomed in tailored pinstripes, his thick moustache and swept back black hair, greying slightly at the quiff, make a confident statement of friendly but no-nonsense authority—which he'd like his employees to share. The minor glitch I'd seen was a part of his challenge to instil greater self-belief in his workforce, he said. 'I think it's a post-colonial legacy, the deferential aspect, the bowing and the scraping and there has to be a balance. I think you come to a point where we like hearing that we are a hospitable nation, and that's good, but are we so hospitable that we break some rules or lower the quality or whatever we're delivering, what is that dividing line?' he asked in a deep baritone.

It is a question of confidence for a people whose own sense of self-worth has been weakened by centuries of subjugation, whose creativity has been sharpened by poverty and scarcity, but who have yet to fully believe in their own potential for greatness, he said.

This is why he dislikes not only the cute compromises of jugaad innovations but also the romanticization of them by commentators in recent years.

His earliest memory of the phenomenon was from trips to Delhi in his early twenties when he and his friends would 'catch a jugaad'—a home-made taxi made from scrap parts of old cars and motorbikes. 'I remember there was a part of a Mahindra jeep also involved, either the transmission or the axle, something that was fitted with the front of a Harley. That was where I first came face-to-face with the word. You go to Delhi and say "I'll catch a jugaad." It was a taxi. That's why I think it [the word] comes from "jorna" [the Hindi verb to join together] because all these disparate elements, scavenged from various vehicles...became a jugaad. If you take that literal meaning, if you go on, there are other meanings of it like make do, jugaad is making do,' he explained. For him making do is a legacy of the first decades of India's independence when scarcity required ingenuity for survival and small comfort. Today, after more than twenty years of economic liberalization, India no longer suffers from scarcity in the same way, but it is still blinkered by a 'making do' outlook.

The jugaads he and his friends caught in Delhi several decades ago still ply the highways of Haryana, Uttar Pradesh, Rajasthan and parts of the capital today, with contemporary bikes replacing the old Harley-Davidson's. Websites celebrating their ingenuity abound and management gurus cite them as examples of frugal innovation, metaphors for 'out- of-the-box' solutions which could save bloated businesses everywhere. But while they were once handy for Anand Mahindra, they are now his idea of a nightmare. 'They're unlicensed, they're unregulated, they spew emissions, they're noisy, they violate every law,' he said. They were once the only option for those who couldn't afford or create better and had to make do with the cast-off junk they had to hand, and for many they still are. What troubles him is that too many Indians take too much pride in them and are too happy to be praised for flawed innovations when they could be creating so much more. He sees the same phenomenon in the satisfaction many take from the story of Mumbai's legendary dabbawalas—the army of semi-literate men from rural Maharashtra's Warkari community who deliver millions of tiffin lunches from the city's wives, mothers and servants to the offices of their husbands, sons and masters through an incomprehensible system of colour-coded handoffs.

Today they also use alphanumeric codes and their operations are said to maintain a Six Sigma rating of 99.9999—they make fewer than one mistake in every six million deliveries. The widespread pride taken in their global recognition reflects a continuing insecurity India must emerge from, Anand Mahindra said, at least if it is ever to lead the world with its innovations rather than make the best of a bad job. 'It's nice when the *New York Times* writes an article on jugaad, about the dabbawalas and how they make do without IT and still have Six Sigma delivery quality and so on, because it says "hey we're not that bad", we can look in the mirror and say what we thought was poverty and scarcity and lack of resources is being praised and [people are saying] "hey you guys are smart". So it was a necessary step as we were engaging with the world to gain self-esteem,' he said.

But its continuing focus on jugaad has hobbled India's progress and left it sweating the small stuff rather than inspiring it to create the world-beating innovations he believes it is capable of. He believes it's a factor in why Indian science has not produced a home-grown Nobel Prize winner since 1930. 'We do need more of them, that's my only argument, that I don't want the romanticization of jugaad to stop us on our journey, I want us to get up and keep going on,' he said. He sees India's lingering low self-esteem as a 'pernicious effect of colonialism' and encourages his own staff to see the value of their own contributions. 'When I go to our shop floor and I talk to workmen and they've come up with something ingenious which is one-tenth what it would cost us if we purchased it from some Western company, some device, I would say "wow, this is interesting, did you guys do this?" and they'd say "yeah, just a bunch of us got together and we found that we were working too hard so we came up with this, using scrap material". And I said, "did you patent this? Because this is very interesting", and they would say "this is just a small thing, what the hell, why should we care?"'

Staff at his German subsidiary, by contrast, filed fifteen patents on cost-saving components during the depth of the 2009 recession. 'It's because they have enough self-esteem that they don't belittle what they do. They walk away and say we've come up with something worth taking on,' he said. Mahindra now holds 'innovation melas' at its Research Valley to encourage all their staff to patent their discoveries.

The challenge, he said, is to persuade Indians to take responsibility for both their failures and their successes. 'My brother has this wonderful imitation he does which he uses to characterize Indian slothfulness, he has a good Maharashtrian accent: "I didn't do it, he did it!",' he said, his arms crossed, each pointing the opposite way and laughing merrily. 'That's what bedevils India. I break up every time... Everybody says "I didn't do it", and the problem is nobody is doing it. They point blame at what doesn't happen but it also happens with the virtuous things. Somebody else is doing it, it's somebody else's job. How do we turn everybody into an innovator?' he asked. He sees progress in his workforce, where staff are beginning to file patents and take greater pride in their own inventions and he sees hope in a new generation with greater expectations than their parents. Half of India's population today is under twenty-five and will not settle for jugaad quality. 'That's the difference between today's India and the old one. In the old India, the leaders thought "Look, it's such a poor country, if we can just get by, if we can make do, that's great". What any future leader of this country has to recognize is that people are not willing to just make do any more. There is going to be a hunger for new levels of material fulfilment and new levels of quality of life and unless we come up with new answers, if we are still scavengers on the beach as opposed to people who are reflecting on new solutions, they're not going to be coming up with the kind of solutions this country needs,' he said.

Will 70 or 80 per cent not be good enough for them? 'You tell me, do you want to take a medicine that's 70 per cent effective? I think that's bogus! Try to imagine a guy who produces 80 per cent quality here, you don't want to be in that 20, right?'

Anand Mahindra's question cut to the chase but he was not alone in posing it. On 26 February 2014, essentially the same question was put at a briefing meeting at the United States Congress by a group of medical experts who voiced serious doubts about the quality and efficacy of cheap 'generic' medicines produced in India and fears that their lapses could prove fatal. Their point was not esoteric. In the last three decades, much of the developed world has come to depend on the cost-savings from using generic versions or copies of Western branded medicines. Indian pharmaceutical companies have grown to meet the great demand for cheap drugs. The drugs provided free or state-subsidized in Britain, the United States or the European Union are courtesy of the billions of dollars saved by buying Indian generics. Regulatory authorities in those and other countries around the world are charged with ensuring that these drugs are exact replicas of their branded equivalents—that they are just as safe and effective and that their production meets the same exacting standards. There are good reasons for this. The slightest deviations or inconsistencies in production or failure to properly record anomalies in test data can lead to adulteration and increase the risk of the tablet or dose being ineffective or toxic—with potentially fatal effects. One of the experts on Capitol Hill, Dinesh Thakur, cited protests in Srinagar, Jammu and Kashmir, in 2013 over the deaths of several hundred children who had allegedly been given adulterated doses of two antibiotics found to be unfit for consumption by the state's drugs control department.

Mr Thakur, an Indian born, United States-trained chemical engineer, had gained a special insight into the scale of adulteration after he joined Ranbaxy, India's biggest producer of generic medicines, as its global head of research in 2003. He discovered some of its medicines, including drugs for heart failure, had been tested at a laboratory alleged to have fabricated data. He turned whistle-blower and took his findings to the US regulator, which launched its own investigation. In May 2013, Ranbaxy USA, Inc. pleaded guilty to several felony charges relating to the adulteration of medicines and was fined a total of $500 million. Mr Thakur was given a $48 million reward as the whistle-blower. His evidence to the United States Food and Drug Administration highlighted adulteration in life-saving drugs, antibiotics and other medicines.

'When companies sell adulterated drugs, they undermine the integrity of the FDA's approval process and may cause patients to take drugs that are substandard, ineffective, or unsafe,' Assistant Attorney for the US Department of Justice Stuart F. Delery said following the settlement.

When Gerald Heddell, head of inspections at Britain's drugs regulator, the Medicines and Healthcare products Regulatory Agency (MHRA) visited India in December 2013, he warned its generic drugs industry—which supplies 20 per cent of all medicines sold in the United Kingdom—that it was in danger of losing public confidence.

One of the generics manufacturers which came under fire was Wockhardt. In July 2013, the MHRA recalled sixteen Wockhardt medicines, including treatments for Parkinson's disease, Alzheimer's, depression, diabetes and high blood pressure, after inspectors found serious flaws at its plant in Aurangabad, Maharashtra. They discovered poor manufacturing and cleaning standards, building defects and 'evidence of forged documents relating to staff training records'.

According to Dinesh Thakur, the Capitol Hill whistle-blower, the problems in the industry were rooted in jugaad thinking and in a fatalism referred to as 'chalta hai'—that's how it goes, the Indian que sera.

Coupled with a deference that prevents good employees questioning their seniors, the two attitudes explained not only the resignation to shoddy work and mismanagement but also 'why we have come to accept poor governance, corruption, incompetence and entitlement as facts of life,' he said. 'There is an implicit understanding that because the solution needs to be quick and creative, it is acceptable to make a compromise on the quality...we have come to accept that if it is 80 per cent good, works 80 per cent of the time, and does 80 per cent of what it needs to do, it is acceptable. This attitude manifests itself in almost every facet of common life in India,' he explained in a commentary in *The Hindu* newspaper shortly after the Ranbaxy judgement.

The impact of India's jugaad approach posed a threat not only to the country's future, but also, potentially, to the lives of patients around the world being treated with its cheap generic drugs. One of Mr Thakur's allies in the campaign to highlight the menace of adulterated medicines is Dr Harry Lever, a leading cardiologist from Cleveland Clinic, one of America's top four hospitals. He had so many patients who had failed to improve after taking Indian generic drugs, including diuretics, beta blockers and anti-cholesterol medicines, that he now had 'clinical suspicions' about them, he said. Their failure had been potentially life-threatening in some cases. 'There are unacceptable problems with drugs coming from India. I have seen patients who are taking diuretics for heart failure who do not get an adequate response and go back into heart failure...I have found if I change the patients to a different generic brand, but keep the dose the same, they respond,' he said in a Capitol Hill briefing. Dr R. Preston Mason, an expert in cardiovascular disease with over 250 scientific publications to his name, outlined the results of his tests to compare generic versions of an anti-cholesterol drug from the United States and the rest of the world, mostly from India, with samples of the original branded medicine. He found 'alarming' levels of impurities in the generic samples from overseas, in some cases of between 10 and 15 per cent, but none in the original drug manufactured by Pfizer. The impurity, he said, was the product of improper manufacturing. While there was no health benefit from the impurity, more tests were needed to establish whether they had any harmful effects on patients. 'The effects of these impurities could be toxic. All we know is that they don't work. Why should we be taking medicines with impurities or contaminants? We don't expect 10 to 15 per cent of apples to be rotten. When we looked at the branded drugs like Pfizer, they had no impurities,' he said later. Roger Bate, a British specialist in fake and adulterated medicines who also addressed the Capitol Hill briefing, said there was evidence that Indian manufacturers were cutting corners to boost profits and that patients should have the right to refuse Indian generics.

Their comments pose a serious challenge to an industry which has not only brought the prospect of cheaper treatment to India, but hope of survival to poor patients throughout the developing world, who cannot afford branded versions of the life-saving drugs they need. It presents a risk to all countries that have come to depend on the vast savings governments make from buying cheap Indian generics. If those countries suddenly had to switch back to branded medicines, could their healthcare budgets afford it? And if they could, would branded manufacturers be able to meet the demand?

At the heart of these scandals, as Dinesh Thakur explained, is not a lack of technical knowhow, but a jugaad mindset of cutting corners, adulteration and skirting the rules to make money. But the production of cheap medicines is not the only part of the Indian healthcare system where bad jugaad is putting lives in jeopardy and India's reputation on the line. The rapid rise of India's pharmaceutical industry has been replicated by the growth of its private medical sector. Its emergence reflected its government's liberalization policies permitting private enterprise in sectors such as healthcare, and the contrast between private hospitals and government ones was already stark when I arrived in India in 2005.

I saw both ends of the spectrum within our first few weeks. When my brother said he'd had a CT scan to check his heart, I decided to have mine checked too. His had cost £500 (₹40,000) back in Britain but the same package was offered at Delhi's Apollo Hospital in Sarita Vihar for one-fifth of the price with an appointment available the following morning. A smugness not unrelated to sibling rivalry set in and it was only intensified by the smartness of the hospital itself when I arrived. A liveried and turbaned doorman welcomed me as our car stopped at the steps. We walked into a canopied lobby fringed with smart shops. An army of uniformed cleaners glided across its shiny floor, continually brushing its tiles to a high gloss.

A few years earlier, when I edited the Scottish edition of the *Sunday Times*, a Chevening scholar on secondment from the *Times of India* had told me that Delhi's private hospitals were far cleaner and more modern than the drug resistant bacteria-infested wards of our Victorian Royal Infirmaries. We ran a story on it in around 2002 as a counter-intuitive controversy, and it appeared to be true. No wonder then that 25 per cent of Apollo patients were foreign 'medical tourists' looking to jump Western waiting lists without breaking the bank.

At the end of the first month in my new job, however, I saw the flip side. On Saturday, 29 October 2005, as millions of Delhiwallas hit the shops to buy last minute gifts for Diwali, two bombs tore through the heaving Paharganj and Sarojini Nagar markets and a third was left on a packed bus in Govindpuri. More than fifty people were killed. The injured were taken to the Ram Manohar Lohia, Lady Hardinge and Safdarjung hospitals, and visiting each of them in a convoy of cars with other journalists that night left indelible memories. The foyers were poorly lit, dirty and abandoned to stray animals: newborn kittens frolicked in one corner, a balding dog with a skin disease and a bitch lay in another. There was a weak scent of urine where I had expected the disciplined smell of disinfectant. The aim was to find the conscious survivors who could recall the scene, the shopping frenzy, the crushing crowds, and then the explosion and carnage. Instead, I took a wrong turn, opened a door I hoped would lead to the waiting families and came face to face with the victims whose story had come to a sudden, brutal end: corpses piled, unceremoniously, one on top of the other in a small storeroom. No liveried doorman in this hospital to welcome the wealthy with a reverential bow, no images which might grace a hoarding or television ad to tempt a 'medical tourist'. The contrast highlighted how India was capable of providing the best but more often delivered much worse to a people resigned to shoddy and insanitary conditions.

Dr Kunal Saha and his psychiatrist wife Anuradha made the same, ultimately tragic, assumption in 1998 after she discovered a rash on her arm while visiting her family in Kolkata. They decided to seek treatment at one of the city's best private hospitals. He was the self-assured son of a doctor, who described himself and his future bride in the style of a *Statesman* newspaper ad for arranged marriages. He was 'six feet tall with typical TDH (tall-dark-handsome) look' with a 'remarkable ability to overcome academic challenges'. Anuradha, a doctor's daughter, was a 'rare combination of angelic beauty and simmering grace' and an 'exceptionally intelligent student'. Theirs was a 'love marriage', they met by chance at a picnic party mainly attended by doctors, fell in love, and moved to a new life in the United States. Kunal found a well-paid assistant professorship at the Ohio State University, Columbus, where they'd bought a lakeside mansion and a Mercedes SUV for the family they were planning. She was thirty-six, he was a year older, and they were about to start living their American dream.

The rash appeared on Anuradha's arm shortly after they returned to Kolkata to seek her mother's blessings and they decided to consult one of the city's leading doctors, Dr Sukumar Mukherjee, at the Nightingale Diagnostic Centre private clinic. However, Anuradha's condition deteriorated and she died of sepsis, barely three weeks after complaining of a minor rash.

Tragic though it is, their story would normally be filed away in dusty, bug-eaten newspaper archives, along with all the other tragedies India suffered in 1998—the Gujarat cyclone which killed more than 1,100 or the Chapnari Massacre in which Kashmiri terrorists killed twenty-five guests at a wedding celebration. What kept it alive was Kunal Saha's fifteen-year campaign to fix accountability for his wife's demise. In October 2013, following a gruelling legal battle in which he represented himself in court, challenged the medical establishment which had trained him, and spent ₹9 crore, Dr Mukherjee was held 'culpable of civil liabilities' along with two doctors at the AMRI hospital. Kunal Saha was awarded ₹11 crore in compensation. It was a remarkable achievement which shocked an Indian medical establishment entirely unaccustomed to accountability: Only 515 complaints were registered against India's 800,000 doctors from 2001 to 2010, of which action was taken against, in fifteen cases according to a Right to Information (RTI) filed by Dr Saha's People for Better Treatment group. For perspective, Britain has around 170,000 registered doctors, 669 of whom were suspended or struck off the medical register between 2007 and 2012. That so few doctors had faced disciplinary action required an RTI application and many months of waiting. According to Dr Saha, its opacity reflects its corruption. 'There is a perception that doctors are not next to God but almost God. You don't question a doctor. In the United States, even with complicated surgery, you draw a picture to give confidence. Here the doctor will only say he's not well, very bad,' he explained. The absence of accountability has created a culture of impunity. 'It's a human psychology. If you steal something but don't get caught, a lot of people will steal and that's what's happening,' he added. Dr Saha now leads the People for Better Treatment campaign to help the families of negligence victims seek justice and to expose corruption in the medical profession. The forces ranged against him, he said, are formidable.

◆

The corruption and greed at the heart of India's medical system has been offered as an explanation for unnecessary surgeries, organ transplants motivated by financial considerations rather than patient care, excessive and unwarranted medical tests requested by doctors who receive kickbacks of up to 50 per cent on each. In one poor farming village in Andhra Pradesh, almost all the adult women had been told they would die if they did not have hysterectomies—their husbands sold their land to pay ₹60,000 for the unnecessary surgery and then left them. 'I can't have children after the hysterectomy so now my husband has abandoned me and married again,' Kondpuram Swaroopa said.

The prescription of medicines, adulterated or otherwise, is often motivated by incentives from unscrupulous drug company representatives. According to Dr Kunal Saha, these reps have become one of the main sources of 'continuing medical education' for overstretched doctors to keep their knowledge up to date from impartial papers. 'Doctors are too busy to study the medical journals because they're seeing 200 patients a day. Who is teaching them? Representatives from pharmaceutical companies—"you will get a trip to Singapore after 100 prescriptions." So he starts writing without reading. They know they will get away with it and no one will hold them accountable,' he said. They operate in the medical grey zone and put a cynical twist on Anil Gupta's 'Indian heuristic' in which '70 per cent is good enough' and 'nature will take care of the rest'.

The culture of impunity in India's medical sector gives rise to certain dubious practices. In January 2014, the *Times of India* quoted a number of doctors lowering costs by using household kitchen equipment and domestic tools as jugaad surgical implements. One revealed he used stationery paper clips instead of surgical clamps while another surgeon said he strained human fat in facial surgery with kitchen sieves. Household cable ties were used as tourniquets. All regarded their 'frugal innovations' as sources of pride.

The extent to which doctors in India have bypassed or flouted the rules and engaged in jugaad practices has eroded the trust of many patients. This was illustrated vividly in 2014 by a British doctor who had worked as a volunteer in a hospital in Himachal Pradesh. In an article in *The BMJ* (formerly called *British Medical Journal*), David

Berger, a district medical officer specializing in emergency medicine, described how he had been told to let a colleague handle the paperwork when he referred a heart patient for an electrocardiogram because it attracted a 10 to 15 per cent commission. The hospital's marketing director would regularly pass on the kickbacks to the doctors in cash. 'Investigations and procedures are abused as a means of milking patients. I saw one patient with no apparent structural heart disease and uncomplicated essential hypertension who had been followed up by a city cardiologist with an echocardiogram every three months, a totally unnecessary investigation. A senior doctor in another hospital a couple of hours away was renowned for using ultrasonography as a profligate, revenue earning procedure, charging desperately poor people ₹1,000 each time. Everyone who works in healthcare in India knows this kind of thing is widespread,' he wrote. 'A common complaint I heard from poor and middle-class people is that they don't trust their doctors. They don't trust them to be competent or to be honest, and they live in fear of having to consult them,' he wrote.

Dr Kunal Saha said the impact of graft in healthcare goes deeper than its effect on the patient–doctor relationship: 'Here corruption is literally human life and death.' It is unknown which of these fates befell Shashi Mohan Kumar, a poor twenty-two-year-old labourer from Bihar, who was left in a coma when the footbridge he and his road gang members were rushing to complete in time for the opening of Delhi's 2010 Commonwealth Games collapsed. The broken bridge symbolized much that was wrong with India in general and the preparations for the games in particular. It was a white laddered steel arch, with a concrete walkway propped high above a new highway, with the new modern sails and beams of the Jawaharlal Nehru Stadium rising up behind it. It rested on rungs but one of them loosened under the weight and the main walking surface snapped at both ends and crashed down on to the road below.

News of the collapse emerged as various national teams arrived in Delhi and voiced their shock at the filthy and dangerous conditions of the athletes' village.

Team Scotland staff arrived early to find their accommodation tower unfinished and described it as 'unsafe and unfit for human habitation'. They discovered a dog fouling one of their beds, broken plumbing and exposed electrical wiring. Photographs of rusty paan stains on the bathroom wall and white sinks caked in brown muck went viral. 'There have been dogs roaming around the village, the apartments are filthy, there are piles of rubble and right now it's not fit to receive 6,500 athletes and officials,' said Michael Cavanagh of Team Scotland.

For Commonwealth Games Federation (CGF) officials it did not come as a surprise. All the works should have been completed a year earlier so games officials could test the readiness of the facilities in time to make good any shortcomings. But despite repeated warnings from CGF executives that the facilities would not be ready, Indian officials appeared unconcerned.

As athletes threatened to withdraw and their coaches demanded last minute improvements, the CGF's chief executive Mike Hooper, a burly, bluff New Zealander, blamed the Indian government. He had inspected the games venues in March 2010, sixths months earlier, and found they were not even close to completion.

I had met Mike Hooper in a restaurant on Delhi's Connaught Place in 2008 for a briefing on the preparations and even then he had the appearance of a man who was at his wits' end. He had with him a huge suitcase and when his wife later joined us for a drink I asked if they were going somewhere nice for a break. They weren't going away, he said. 'Why the suitcase?' I asked. 'That's my office,' he replied. Indian officials had evicted him from his office and he was forced to carry all his paperwork on their progress in a wheelie trunk.

A year later, his boss, Michael Fennell, the games' president, had vented his disappointment with the Indian government's failure to meet construction deadlines for the games' opening the following year. Only six of nineteen venues were on track. 'With only a year to run until the games, I feel I must personally brief the prime minister of India on the lack of preparations and to seek his input... The preparations for the games are significantly behind, so much so that the CGF is extremely worried about the organizing committee's ability to deliver the games to any comparable standard to that of the last two editions [Manchester and Melbourne],' he warned.

Pressure cascaded down from the office of Manmohan Singh, the prime minister, to his ministers, their secretaries, organizing committee members, and finally to the contractors and their poor migrant labourers. The preparations now proceeded at breakneck speed, but the haste also led to unfortunate consequences. Shashi Mohan Kumar and his twenty-six workmates became the victims of one such tragedy.

I found him in a ward at the All India Institute of Medical Sciences (AIIMS), India's most prestigious government hospital, where he was lying unconscious and attended only by his teenage brother, who had travelled from their home in Bihar to look after him. A pinched and freshly stitched mauve scar snaked across the back of his shaved head.

His doctor seemed oblivious to his condition, and when I asked him why he had been neglected in this fashion he said it wasn't the hospital's job to keep him clean, even if being in a coma left him immobile and vulnerable to sores and infections that could kill him. He would, in all likelihood, die anyway, his doctor, Ajay Singh, told me.

If he survived the first fifteen days, he would be sent back to his village in Muzaffarpur district where his breathing and feeding tubes would have to be cleaned every three hours. It would be impossible there for his wounds to be kept clean and he would succumb to a fatal infection. 'In the village he has no chance, he will die,' he said.

Had Indian officials put in place a clear command and management structure in sufficient time, there may not have been the last-minute frenzy of construction work and Shashi Mohan Kumar may not have had to suffer.

But, according to the CGF chief, Mike Hooper, the wider crisis, in which the bridge collapse was just one event, was almost wilful.

'All the warning signs were there. We were pushing very hard, we kept pushing. You can lead a horse to water you can't make it drink. These people just did not understand, or seem to accept the magnitude of the problem...There were consistently missed deadlines. The government agencies have let everybody down,' he said.

His analysis was borne out by then Comptroller and Auditor General Vinod Rai. The delays which made the preparations a last-minute frenzy of corner cutting had been part of a deliberate attempt to create a sense of emergency in which the normal procedures could be bypassed and favoured contractors hired under 'force majeure', he found.

The report is worth quoting in full because it captures the absurdity that more planning may have gone into engineering a lucrative final year crisis than in the preparations to stage the games.

> The processing of certain sensitive contracts was allocated in an arbitrary and ad hoc manner to certain officials with the concerned functional areas. Such action diluted the process of due diligence and scrutiny. There was enormous bunching of high value contacts in 2010 particularly in the second and third quarters. The argument of urgency was used to obviate the regular processes of tendering for award of contracts. We found numerous instances of single tendering award of 'nomination basis' contracts to ineligible vendors, inconsistent use of restrictive pre-qualification conditions (PQ) to limit competition to favour certain vendors.

'Basically,' he explained to me later, shortly after he had retired as Comptroller and Auditor General, 'it was left to the eleventh hour to circumvent procedures and then to give contracts to your own nominees.'

India's prime ministers, first Atal Bihari Vajpayee and then Dr Manmohan Singh, may have wanted to showcase India's rapid development and new capability, but the officials actually organizing the event were prepared to have India humiliated before the world to benefit their mates.

Why would they take such a gamble when the stakes were so high?

'What happens is "I have to complete it, I have to rush through, if I have to rush through I have to cut procedures, I'll commit irregularities, hopefully these irregularities will be masked by the fact that I'm short of time." That's a risk and reward phenomenon, now in doing so, those of us who [are] amenable to acts of commission, which means for personal benefit, they fall prey to this: "Okay, I'm going to spend ₹100, they should be spent in a certain way, I'm short circuiting that because I've no time and I have emergency powers. This ₹100, how I spend it is entirely my choice",' Vinod Rai explained.

In his own visits to the games sites, he saw evidence of jugaad decisions and hasty, shoddy work everywhere, but especially in the athletes' village.

In a later speech to the Bhubaneswar branch of the Indian Institute of Professional Managers, he explained how corruption and shoddiness, which had characterized the Commonwealth Games preparations, had reflected the hold jugaad has over the Indian mindset. It needs to be banished and replaced by a habit of excellence, he argued.

India's reaction to winning its highest ever Olympic medal haul in 2012—two silvers and four bronzes—was a case in point, he said. Despite the poor showing, and the fact that not a single athlete from the world's second most populated nation could pose biting into a gold medal, the tiny band of 'winners' returned to India as conquering heroes. They were garlanded with marigolds, showered with petals, paraded on open-top buses and given cheques and plots of land by their chief ministers.

China, by contrast, the country India is competing with for the tag of the world's fastest growing major economy, won thirty-eight golds, twenty-seven silvers and twenty-three bronze medals, a tally of eighty-eight—eighty-two more than India.

The poor return was an indictment of a government that hadn't provided the encouragement and training facilities necessary for success. It also reflected a deeper malaise, he said: 'When the world goes for gold, do we settle for bronze? Are we content to be a nation of mediocres? Are we content to celebrate mediocrity? Has mediocrity become the nation's soul?' he asked.

The questions were heartfelt, pitched from a lifetime of devotion and disappointment in India's elite civil service and reflected a deeply wounded pride that a country with so much human talent and abundant raw materials had achieved so little. He bristled at being quizzed at international conferences over how India had the world's fourth highest number of billionaires but the most children suffering with malnutrition.

'It reflects on how good we are as administrators, scientists and educationists. It reflects on us as we have become a land of jugaad. We excel in cut and paste solutions. We make promises and provide quick fix solutions to tide over the crisis at hand thereby abandoning the long-term objective,' he explained.

He himself had seen the corrupt side of jugaad in his earlier years as a civil servant in the government's excise department where the honesty of an officer was rated by his willingness to take his fair share of the hafta, the weekly kickbacks for speedy shipment clearances or licences, but no more than that. Corrupt was normal, greedy and corrupt was underhand and reprehensible.

It reminded me of a story an Indian businessman had told me about a meeting he'd had with a chief minister who had called together all the companies interested in bidding for a power plant contract. In front of the bidders, and his civil servants, he explained that there would be a minimum kickback at the outset of several million dollars. 'It was seen as a mark of his honesty that he fixed the amount before his babus,' the businessman explained.

My yatra had entered a darker landscape—the innocent optimism of my Snowbreeze and the rakish joy of my billionaire traders were a long way behind me. I began with the frugal innovations of heroes who wanted to change the world but now I was mired with sordid stories of political, professional and administrative corruption.

Can these heroes and villains really be connected? Are they both practitioners of jugaad? And if they are, is the word itself not a non-sense?

A friend had raised the question when I'd explained my jugaad journey to him, in particular in relation to corruption. 'Surely, sometimes corruption is just corruption?' he asked.

Of course, sometimes corruption is just that. But in India the term jugaad is used freely for both the good and bad, for frugal innovations and corrupt practices, often without a moral distinction between the two. It relates to the improvisation required in difficult circumstances to find a solution. The end may be selfless, community-minded, selfish or venal but the lateral thinking involved is referred to as jugaad in any case.

To work around conventional wisdom on what can be done with what materials to what standard, or to bypass rules and laws—both involve a subversive way of thinking.

An honest colleague highlighted the blurred distinction when he asked if I would like an Indian driving licence.

They were said to be difficult for foreigners to get, but he knew someone who could arrange it for around ₹3,000. 'They're for sale?' I asked naively. 'Sure,' he replied. What about taking a driving test? 'You can,' he replied. 'You take the test and you fail. You say to the examiner "can you do some jugaad for me?" and then he says "Okay, give me ₹3,000".' The bribe is the reason why the corrupt official deploys jugaad thinking to bypass the law and turn the paperwork of failure into a certificate of success.

One is process, the other purpose, but they have become fused in modern usage. The lateral thinking involved in delaying the award of Commonwealth Games contracts and the kickbacks allegedly demanded and paid to secure them are now synonymous—jugaad.

According to Vinod Rai, the failures of India's athletes, contractors and officials all reflect the hold jugaad thinking has in government.

'A reason for our lack of excellence in performance is because we do not choose the best. There is no transparency in our procedures. No integrity in our professionalism. Lack of such ethical practice leads to lack of good governance,' he said.

Ethics and integrity were at the heart of the problem, he later told me. Only 40 per cent of Indians, perhaps 50 at a push, are honest 'people in white who would never do something irregular'. 30 per cent 'are in black', dishonest and 'looking for opportunities all the time'. 25 per cent are 'fence sitters' in grey 'which means when the opportunity comes their way they might fall prey to it'.

The legacy of these 'quantums' is strewn across the landscape, but heavily concentrated in the capital, Delhi, where an estimated ₹28,000 crore was spent on the Commonwealth Games to change the way the world thought of India and leave its own people with world class sporting facilities.

In July 2013, I returned to the scene of Bharatbala's triumphant opening ceremony at the Jawaharlal Nehru Stadium to see how well the sporting legacy was holding up.

If you had to date its construction based on what I saw, you'd have said perhaps two decades earlier. Concrete cladding on the staircases had fallen away, light fittings, marble steps were chipped, and lights which were supposed to be flush with the ceiling hung down from exposed electric wires. The stands had been commandeered by street dogs. A television or light control room high up in the bleachers had been completely warped by monsoon rains—unsealed plasterboard panels bulged out and glass panels to keep it weathertight were missing.

One of the few things intact was the black marble plaque to mark the opening of the stadium which was 'dedicated to the nation' by the then sports minister, Dr Manohar Singh Gill, and then chief minister of Delhi, Sheila Dikshit. A grinning, larger than life-sized model of Sher, the Games' tiger mascot, alongside the plaque, emphasized the irony.

This was what remained of India's best effort to change the world's mind on how far it had come in its development, and this was what Shashi Mohan Kumar had given his health and future for.

What had become of him? Did Delhi's government ever pay out the compensation it had promised to him, or his family if he didn't survive? Did he ever make it back to his village in Bihar or survive the two weeks his doctor predicted he would live before village squalor polished him off?

He had long since been forgotten. The former labour minister, who like his Congress colleagues were swept from power by the anti-corruption Aam Aadmi Party (AAP) in the December 2013 elections, had no information.

The staff on the ward at AIIMS where he once laid unconscious and neglected also had no recollection of him. He may have lived, he may have died, but his fate wasn't worth recording.

Like Anuradha Saha, he was unfortunate to be at the wrong side of the Indian heuristic, beyond the '70 per is good enough' cut-off and condemned to the 30 per cent that bad jugaad leaves for nature to take care of.

CHAPTER 6

A RIVER RUNS THROUGH IT

In February 2013, the largest religious gathering on earth assembled for the Kumbh Mela at Allahabad's Sangam, the confluence of Hinduism's two holiest rivers, the Ganga and Yamuna, to praise the gods where their nectar fell on earth. Along with Haridwar, Nashik and Ujjain, it is one of the faith's most revered spots, and tens of millions of pilgrims descend upon them in turn every three years to pray, bathe in the holy waters and purify themselves. This particular year's mela was special, not just a triennial kumbh but a once in every 144 years Mahakumbh. Never in history has there been a quest for purity on this scale. More than 100 million Hindus—one in every twelve of the world's second largest nation—gathered in a makeshift metropolis two and a half times the size of Tokyo and five times the size of Mumbai. Every day, hundreds of thousands poured in on chartered buses, trains and even executive jets. The rich were driven in SUVs to their luxury resorts, the great masses trudged their head-load to canvas tent suburbs to sleep on straw, while the poorest huddled down on the muddy roadsides and shivered together under heaps of blankets in the freezing winter fog. A vast bamboo metropolis of hotels, huts, shopping malls, hospitals and police stations was built around dirt roads and pontoon bridges in just three months—from the end of the monsoon at the beginning of October to January, when the first pilgrims immersed themselves in the water.

I arrived there six weeks into the festival for the Maghi Purnima

Snan, one of the four main bathing days, when ten million people were expected to immerse their bodies in the hope of washing away their sins.

I woke at 4 a.m., shivering in a mosquito-infested government hut and joined an endless procession of shivering souls, shuffling slowly down the redemption dirt track under harsh temporary street lights. Many walked barefoot with their heads and chests wrapped in winter shawls for warmth. Daybreak backlit the horizon and exposed the hunched silhouettes of hundreds of men squatting down for their morning ablutions.

Open defecation is a major problem in India. According to the World Health Organization, one billion people around the globe have no access to a toilet and almost 600 million of them live in India. The resultant poor hygiene is to blame for the deaths of 750,000 children under five who die every year from diarrhoea-related illnesses and almost half of these tragedies—334,000—are in India. According to the leading environmentalist Sunita Narain, 'India is drowning in its own excreta.'

More Indians own mobile phones than have access to a toilet, a fact which has shamed some of the country's leaders and left its women, and occasionally its men, highly vulnerable. Some of the rapes and murders that have caused outrage in recent years have been perpetrated against women and girls who'd gone to relieve themselves in nearby fields or forests. Men have been attacked by tigers and leopards. In one particularly sad case, twenty-one-year-old Vijay Singh was killed and eaten by a man-eating tigress in Uttar Pradesh's Moradabad district on the day before his wedding in December 2013. As he squatted down near his village pond, watching a video on his phone to pass the time, the tigress pounced. Relatives searching for him followed a trail of blood from the phone and found his remaining bones in a nearby sugar cane field.

For anyone who has lived in India, the sight of children straining astride an open sewer pipe or men on their haunches along the railway sidings is unremarkable. The Mahakumbh, however, brought the problem into stark relief. Open defecation was a major issue here. Much of the waste had leached its way into the Yamuna and Ganga rivers despite the government's best efforts. Officials had reduced upstream human waste and chemical effluent in the four months before the Mahakumbh. But tests carried out after the first bathing day found organic pollution at more than double the acceptable level. That was at its cleanest point in the great gathering, with two months and ninety million more people yet to arrive.

By the time I reached five weeks later, the river water was decidedly sludgy with a surface scum of wilted puja marigolds, bobbing coconuts, plastic food bags and 'organic matter'. Among the millions of devotees and dreadlocked sadhus was Swami Chidanand Saraswati, one of India's high profile gurus, who has dedicated himself to saving the holy Ganga from its own 'worshippers'. I found him in his sprawling bamboo ashram with its pitched thatch assembly hall and baize-carpeted reception rooms and waited for an audience as ministers and other VIPs queued for a place in his aura. They bowed before him and posed for pictures in front of his campaigning banner: 'Ganga's Rights Are Our Rights'. The withered, saffron-robed guru's global appeal was underscored when he garlanded Prince Charles and the Duchess of Cornwall at his candlelit aarti ceremony on the banks of the Ganga at Haridwar later that year. When the VIPs had taken his blessings, he took me to a quiet corner and explained that the Ganga's state reflected that of the nation and must be restored to the condition its Creator had intended. Those who live along its course, villagers, farmers, industrialists and officials, are all to blame and all of them must be involved in cleaning it, he said. Their faith and India's laws demanded they protect its holiest river from pollution. Its slow death is a national crisis, he explained.

'If the Ganga thrives India thrives, if it dies, India dies. We have to work together because this water is not mere water. There have been laws to protect the Ganga since 1974, but nothing has been done. [The issue is] solid waste management. Sewage and river should not be together... People clean their own homes, why not the streets and the village and the village river? If the village river is clean, the Ganga is clean,' he said.

Yet despite the pollution in its waters, he still bathes in the river every day. 'Water may be dirty but the Ganga is pure. If someone throws something at Mother, you just wash the clothes. Mother does not become dirty. Purity never ends. It's always here. People come to bathe in that purity, that's why there are so many people here. The Kumbh Mela is bringing the awareness. What's the point of coming, having one dip in the holy river, if you don't take care of the river? Everything is lost. If you worship the creator you have to take care of the creation also. It's a beautiful creation,' he said. I considered his 'water is dirty, Ganga is pure' mantra as I watched the sunset over the Sangam from a rowing boat while crossing back past Emperor Akbar's imposing Mughal fort to the opposite shore. It *is* a beautiful creation, but has the ability to see purity in filth made people believe the river doesn't need protection—that it will always cleanse no matter how much waste and toxic chemicals are dumped in it?

The really alarming fact about the Mahakumbh's impact on the river and its banks is that the soiled landscape I saw could have been far worse. In preparation for the Mahakumbh, Uttar Pradesh officials had pumped more water into the river to ensure the waste was washed away faster; there was a crackdown on upstream industries and careful consideration was given to public health in the knowledge that a hundred million people would be living here together spread over a two-month period.

Dr Suresh Dwivedi introduced himself as the chief medical superintendent of Allahabad's Tej Bahadur Sapru Hospital and said it was his third Kumbh Mela but the first that he'd been in charge of health and sanitation. The open-air toilets we were standing amid were public health policy in action, he explained. 'Three crore came on the 10th [of February], so many people, but the area is so clean. Not less than 10 crores [overall]. We've set up fourteen 20-bedded hospitals and one 100 bedded. We've treated 3 lakhs mainly for respiratory tract infections because of the weather and old age problems. Thirty-five thousand [toilets] have been installed... So many people have taken baths, people are drinking the water but we are not seeing any disease. Still the quality is good. Otherwise you would have had a lot of patients in the hospitals,' he said. He and his officials had anticipated the volume of waste that was about to be dumped on their temporary metropolis and took action. They dug pits, poured in insecticides and then, when full, covered them over and left the bacteria to do its work. 'After three months it is harmless sludge. A lot of nitrogen is there which adds to the fertility of the soil,' he explained. The surrounding landscape may have looked like evidence of Sunita Narain's claim that India is drowning in its own waste, but here, for now at least, Dr Suresh Dwivedi was right. Public health planning had accommodated 100 million temporary inhabitants without major disease outbreaks while keeping organic matter in the river down to just double the acceptable levels.

The real threat is from the jugaad governance which is slowly killing these holy rivers between the 144-yearly Mahakumbh melas. Seventy-five miles downstream from the Sangam the combined human, industrial and chemical waste of Delhi, Agra, Kanpur, Allahabad, flows into Varanasi, one of India's holiest pilgrimage destinations, where it mingles with the effluent and sewage of the city's own 3.5 million people.

A further 150,000 visitors arrive here every day. Varanasi is so revered and its pilgrims in such a state of exaltation that the condition of the toxic river seems to many a trivial earthly matter. When Narendra Modi became prime minister after his landslide victory in May 2014, the 'Clean Ganga' programme was professed as an important priority for his government. He successfully fought the Varanasi constituency against Arvind Kejriwal, the activist-turned-leader of the Aam Aadmi Party, and his first act as prime minister was to offer thanks on the banks of the Ganga.

As he did so, he also gave India a stern telling off over the state of its rivers and streets.

'It's with small chores that big goals are accomplished. People must be thinking: "why is this person speaking of garbage?" But that can change India… Cleaning our surroundings is also one way of serving Mother India. You have to do it, we all have to do it together,' he said. It would also have to be done urgently—by the 150th anniversary of Mahatma Gandhi's birth in 2019.

I travelled to Varanasi a few days later to look at the scale of the task India's formidable new prime minister had set both himself and the nation. It was daunting. At Chousatti Ghat, a once grand villa at the river's edge, thick electric cables tumbled down over colonnaded verandas with thick, luxuriant bushes sprouting from gaps in its finely carved masonry. Pink steel doors to the basement godown hung off the hinges. A handsome sandstone arch up on the first floor was in use as a grazing area for goats, but the wire for the pen had snapped and the cloven-hoofed beast was now the king of the terrace. A sewer underneath the building had carved its own channel through the grey beach to pour waste directly into the river. There were red plastic nappy sacks, discarded takeaway bags, disposable cups and water bottles floating in along with other kinds of waste. At the neighbouring Raja Ghat, a cow herder had made a cattle shed from bamboo poles, rusted corrugated iron sheets and a plastic tarpaulin sagging under the weight of monsoon rain. A few feet away the rest of the herd sat at the bottom of a thirty feet-high mound of mud enmeshed with household garbage.

The task of making the Prime Minister's sparkling vision for Varanasi a reality rests on the broad shoulders of Ram Gopal Mohale, his party colleague and city mayor. Where will he start? How had such a revered city been so neglected and soiled by its own worshippers? He blamed the rival Samajwadi Party, then in power in the state, and the Congress Party at the centre for neglecting the city. Neither would loosen the purse strings, he said, and he had been left with responsibility but no power to clean up the mess. Varanasi's sanitation system dates back 500 years to the Mughal empire and today serves a city which pours 300 million litres of sewage into the river. Only

100 million litres of it is treated. Five hundred million tonnes of rubbish is simply dumped, he said.

Now, with Narendra Modi as the city's champion, things will change. Reclining in his armchair, his pale green cotton kurta and lime linen Punjabi waistcoat straining at his paunch, Mr Mohale explained that Mr Modi will not only clean the city but build flyovers and five-star hotels and regenerate its famous Benares silk industry. He will reinvigorate the arts in a city celebrated for icons like Ravi Shankar and Bismillah Khan. 'His vision is to make Varanasi the intellectual and cultural capital of the country,' he said. He certainly wanted to contrast Narendra Modi's passion for reviving the city with the previous government's waste and corruption. I should go to the waste management site on the outskirts of the city to see for myself, he suggested.

A hand-painted but heavily rusted sign said the project had been launched in August 2010 with ₹48 crores from the Union Urban Development Ministry. But there were no indications that it had ever been functional. Several expensive garbage trucks, dumpers and tractors that seemed to be relatively new, had sunk into the mud and were now trapped. Their doors and windows had been left open to the monsoon rains. There were more than a dozen abandoned new vehicles which had been left in the care of a dozing guard. There were piles of smoking rubbish stretching across the horizon but none of the machines under a new steel canopy were working.

Rajiv Gandhi, the late Congress prime minister, had, like Mr Modi, promised to clean up the river and city in 1986 and had earmarked ₹1,700 crore for the Ganga Action Plan. But according to one local political leader, less than a third of the money promised to clean the Ganges had actually been spent on it while as much as 70 per cent had been 'siphoned off' by officials and politicians.

The same problem of river pollution is very much in evidence in Delhi as well, 400 miles upriver from the Sangam, on the banks of the holy Yamuna. The Yamuna is revered as the living Goddess Yami, daughter of Surya, the Sun God, and the saviour of the newborn Lord Krishna. On the day Krishna was born, his father Vasudeva learned that his uncle, the king, had planned to kill him. He fled carrying the infant God in a basket until they reached the banks of the Yamuna. Its turbulent flood waters were too dangerous to cross but just as they seemed trapped, the river parted to speed them on their way.

For many the Yamuna has the same cleansing properties as the Ganga and its holiest spot is at Nigambodh Ghat, just behind Shah Jahan's Red Fort in the old Walled City. According to Indian folk legend, Lord Brahma, the Creator, had bathed in its waters here to recover the four Vedas he'd forgotten. The ghats themselves are said to have been established by Yudhisthira, the righteous king of Indraprastha, eldest of the good Pandava brothers who eventually defeated their Kaurava cousins in the Mahabharata. Today it is home to one of Delhi's busiest crematoriums and the Yamuna's most polluted stretches. More than sixty bodies are burned here every day on wooden pyres. The black tide makes a sombre backdrop for the saffron flames and the floral scent of sandalwood is overpowered by the choking stench of the dying river. An old labourer carries the ashes in a steel bowl on his head and empties them into the shallows while a young man wading up to his waist hoes them on south towards the greater beyond. The mourners do not seem to be upset by the pollution, just saddened with grief and focused on their religious duty to send their loved one on to their next abode. The same metaphysical separation which keeps the Ganga pure while its waters are rank seems to apply.

The condition of the water itself seemed to reflect Professor Michael Faraday's 1855 description of the River Thames as London headed for the Great Stink in similar circumstances. As his boat steamed from London to Hungerford Bridge he was seized by the stench of its 'opaque pale brown fluid'. He dropped white cards and watched them disappear in the sludge in seconds. 'Near the bridges the feculence rolled up in clouds so dense they were visible at the surface...the whole river was for the time a real sewer,' he wrote.

Today, more than 150 years later, Sunita Narain of Delhi's Centre for Science and Environment (CSE) has inherited Faraday's mantle. Her pungently-titled 2012 report *Excreta Matters* is the contemporary indictment of India's chronic pollution that the professor's white cards and letter to *The Times* were in 1855. It is a study of how 'urban India is soaking up water, polluting rivers and drowning in its own waste,' a 71 city 'geography of shit' to explain the 'political economy of defecation'. Her claim is laid out in stark figures. India's main Class One and Class Two cities produce 38,255 million litres per day (MLD) of sewage, they have the capacity to treat 11,788 MLD but only 8,251 are actually processed. India is being submerged in 30,000 million litres of foaming sewage which poison its rivers every day.

The causes are most concentrated in Delhi, one of the world's most polluted cities. From its royal proclamation as the British raj's new capital at the 1911 Delhi Durbar, its population has grown exponentially. It doubled after Partition in 1947 as Hindu and Sikh refugees from Pakistan flooded across the Punjab and increased tenfold to more than seventeen million in the following years. The capital's planners, however, failed to keep pace with its growth. Today's megacity has seventeen sewage treatment plants to clean the waste of those seventeen million people, but only half of the city's land is covered by the waste pipe network. In 2011, the city generated 4,456 million litres of waste per day while its treatment plants had the capacity to treat only 2,330. In fact they only managed to process 1,478 MLD, leaving just under 3,000 MLD of sewage flowing into the Yamuna.

Delhi's rise has seen the spread of illegal jhuggi settlements of migrant labourers and their families who have moved to the capital in search of work and a better life. There are now believed to be 1,600 of these makeshift shanties throughout the Trans-Yamuna area, while half the population of Delhi live in slums and unauthorized colonies. A 2009 survey of slums throughout India found more than half had open sewers while almost a quarter had none at all.

But despite the squalor they suffer, the poor of India's slums are only a minor contributor to the problem—they generate just 5 per cent of waste because they have so little water. In Delhi, it is the officials and politicians who hog the water—those powerful people in the exclusive Lutyens Bungalow Zone of New Delhi enjoy 462 litres per capita per day compared with just 29 in the Mehrauli area.

Sunita Narain's concern is how much waste will Delhi produce and fail to treat when economic growth lifts its millions of poor 'up the toilet-sewage ladder'. The unlikeliest scenario is that it will be processed and cleansed by the city's seventeen sewage treatment plants. Only three of them function at capacity, and one, at Najafgarh, managed only 4 per cent. The shortfall reflects the government's failure to plan for the city's expansion by connecting new pipes to its spreading population. In the absence of planning, people find their own improvised jugaad solutions. The unconnected slum dwellers either defecate in the open, in small areas of wasteland or on the roadside, or directly into the open drains many of their slums are built alongside. Richer Dilliwalas fortunate enough to be connected to the sewage network are in a slightly better position but cannot entirely escape the reality of a city which reflects their own narrow concerns. Many of the pipes connected to their homes and flush toilets are blocked with tonnes of silt and dust which is why, even in some of the capital's posh colonies, roads turn into open drains when the sewage has nowhere to go.

In our colony, a small and lower middle-class neighbourhood built in the 1950s for refugees from Pakistan, the storm water drain outside our house occasionally overflows because the pipe is blocked solid. The local authority sweepers shunt all the dust into its drains, causing them to silt up and overflow during the monsoon months. On fierce summer days, when the water supply is scarce, tempers fray and some of my neighbours fight over who has been using electric pumps to grab more than their fair share. The wealthy of South Delhi have large storage tanks, powerful pumps to fill them faster than their neighbours when the restricted corporation water flows for only an hour in the morning and again in the afternoon.

Some of them also have tube-wells to draw groundwater when the official supply dries up completely.

When that happens, members of the city's 'tanker mafia' sell their own illegal supplies, drawn from farmhouse wells on the edge of the city, to the desperate. Jugaad quick fixes like these are being made on every street and at every level to grab all you can and look after your own. Nobody trusts the system to deal with these problems and so everyone is looking out for themselves, finding their own private solutions.

Campaigners to save the Yamuna say politicians, officials and business owners take the same approach. A good example of how all of these collude for their own benefit and bypass the laws emerged in July 2013 when a magistrate was suspended for inciting communal tension by demolishing the wall of an under-construction mosque. But the real reason for her suspension, it was alleged, was her role in leading a campaign to stop illegal sand mining damaging the banks of the Yamuna.

Durga Shakti Nagpal established a special investigation and enforcement team to challenge the 'sand mafia' mining the Yamuna and its Hindon tributary in the Noida area just outside the capital in Uttar Pradesh. She had arrested several of its key figures, seized twenty-four dumper trucks and 300 trolleys used to move the sand and was starting to disrupt an illegal business estimated to generate ₹2,000 crore per year. Campaigners say the mining is done in defiance of a Supreme Court order and has now changed the course of the river, destabilized its bed in several places and increased the flood risk to several of Noida's districts. Her campaign however had challenged organized crime gangs which had friends in high places and customers in the capital's booming construction industry who were desperate for their contraband sand. Later, a video emerged of a senior political leader belonging to the ruling party in the state purportedly boasting he had used his influence to have her suspended within forty-one minutes of complaining to the chief minister. His colleague and then fellow cabinet minister, Azam Khan, supported her suspension and said all should fill their boots without impediment: 'Everyone has the right on nature's bounty. Loot as much as you can,' he said.

The *Times of India* said her suspension was a 'loud and clear' message from the state government to all honest civil servants and that she was being punished for 'taking on the sand mafia'.

A year later, the *Mail Today* newspaper returned to Yamuna River bank in Noida to find the villages had taken Azam Khan's message to heart and that the local police were standing guard to make sure they were allowed to dig out the river's bed without interruption. Tractor drivers said they were taking a load for ₹2,800 and selling it for ₹8,500. In Gharbhara village alone half of the people were involved in sand-mining and locals said 700 dumper trucks fill up with sand from the Yamuna's bed there every night.

The water flowing over this disappearing sand into Noida is mainly sewage despite the construction of the Yamunanagar treatment plant a little upstream to keep it clean. According to the Centre for Science and Environment, the plant runs at just 40 per cent capacity but for no benefit at all to the river or its inhabitants. An inspection by the Environmental Pollution (Control and Prevention) Authority in 2006 discovered that all the water treated by the plant was channelled straight back into the river upstream, just before a drain where it is mixed with household sewage and industrial waste before it is picked up again by the treatment plant. Three years later it had yet to stop the madness and officials have yet to offer a rational explanation for it.

Himanshu Thakkar of the South Asia Network on Dams, Rivers and People (SANDRP) believes it's too kind to categorize the corruption of officials and politicians responsible for Delhi's mess as jugaad—he doesn't want to contaminate a word which also covers a lot of good creative thinking. 'But I see it is there in a major way in India,' he said, 'an attempt to cut corners to achieve what you want...the law forbids something, you are ready to bypass the law to get ahead and achieve what you want to achieve.'

It is there too in their acts of omission, their failure to enforce the 1974 Water Pollution Act which forbids pumping sewage into the river. 'This was unlawful but none of these bodies took steps. They're not doing their jobs. They're getting away with not doing what they are supposed to do because there is no accountability, no consequences to ensure it. Corruption comes in many ways. One description is if you don't do what you are paid to do. Another is that they don't want to take any measures which will not pay them some extra money, even though it must lead to improvement in the situation, if it involves extra commitment and effort.

'Corruption plays a role in the functioning of the Sewage Treatment Plants. Some of the money which was supposed to be used for proper functioning is pocketed in an illegal, corrupt way leading to this kind of situation. This is why they [sewage treatment officials] are not able to manage [to do their jobs]; a lot of the money gets pocketed,' he explained.

Delhi has an environmental department, a pollution control board and two central government bodies to ensure the Water Pollution Act is enforced, but 'this all happens right under their noses,' he said.

Officials also turned a blind eye to the rise of 1,600 illegal jhuggis throughout the Trans-Yamuna area which contribute to the pollution of the river. Instead of intervening, a number of government agencies sat back and allowed their builders to construct and sell them. 'Unauthorized colonies don't come up overnight. Various agencies knew,' he said.

But while unauthorized colonies and jhuggies were springing up and channelling their waste into the river, the same officials turning a blind eye to them were also spending vast amounts of money the government had set aside to clean up the pollution—more than ₹6,000 crore in two decades. 'The Yamuna is dirtier than ever even after spending a huge amount…6,500 crores has already been spent to clean the river…by now the Yamuna's water—polluted and black—should have been cleaner,' the Indian parliament's Standing Committee on Urban Development reported in February 2014.

Where did the money go? Manoj Misra of the Yamuna Jiye

Abhiyaan said it was spent to suit corrupt officials rather than clean the river. 'The thousands of crores of rupees spent on cleaning the river have been lost to corruption and wasted on activities where the kickbacks are good,' he said. 'In our work, jugaad plays its [part] in short circuiting the system. Pollution control boards, the system of checks and balances, where you are supposed to adhere to laws and regulations. Especially relating to Water Act and Air Act and Environmental Protection Act,' he explained.

When Jairam Ramesh was appointed environment minister in 2009, there was good cause for hope that officials might start doing their jobs and enforcing the laws. Between then and 2011 and later from 2011 until 2014 as rural development minister, he waged a guerrilla campaign within the government and beyond to enforce these circumvented laws and create a national debate about sanitation. He caused consternation among the country's industrialists by issuing show-cause notices to force them to explain why they were polluting rivers in breach of environmental laws. He described India's beloved railway network as the world's biggest 'open air toilet' and berated its people who cared more about building temples than WCs. He waged a 'no toilet, no bride' campaign to persuade women to reject grooms unless their homes had their own bathroom.

His greatest challenge, Jairam Ramesh said, was the absence of a compliance culture and he set about creating one. He doesn't like the use of the term jugaad to romanticize 'inefficiency or corruption by bypassing rules, regulations'—he wants it to be used positively for frugal innovations—but bringing polluting industrialists who were breaking laws and short-circuiting the enforcement system was one of his key priorities. 'It's straightforward dumping of muck. It's breaking all the rules, not having a sewage control system, the failure to implement standards...The culture of compliance is not there. There's no penalty for non-compliance. The costs of non-compliance are not high. Why does an Indian spit out of his car window but the same Indian who goes to Singapore will not do so? The same Indian who goes to Singapore will follow the laws but when he comes back to

India will not follow the laws. Why? The culture of non-compliance, not enough penalty for non-compliance,' he explained. He waged a campaign to make polluters pay. 'We issued show-cause notices and closure orders on industries which are polluting the rivers for the first time, we issued closure notices to bring a culture of compliance. It worked to the extent that the guys who were polluting didn't pollute and a message did go around that laws are not to be monkeyed with. The laws are meant to be followed,' he said.

Had his campaign survived his move to the Rural Development Ministry? He couldn't say. What did he suspect? 'It may have gone back to business as before,' he conceded.

He was right. In March 2016, one of the country's most popular religious gurus, Sri Sri Ravi Shankar, was allowed to build over more than 1,000 acres on the Yamuna's river bank for a three-day Indian 'cultural Olympics'.

CHAPTER 7

THE GRAND TRUNK ROAD
TO NOWHERE

'Caution and Care
Make Accidents Rare'

The Grand Trunk Road spans more than 2,000 years of history and 2,500 kilometres from Chittagong in Bangladesh to Kabul in Afghanistan.

It links Kolkata on the banks of the Hooghly, a distributary of the holy Ganga, with Varanasi, Hinduism's sacred city, and Allahabad, home of the great Sangam where the Ganga meets the Yamuna. It follows the Yamuna north to Delhi and up through Haryana and Punjab to Amritsar, home of the Golden Temple, the centre of the Sikh faith, and over the Wagah Border to Lahore in Pakistan.

From the capital of the former Sikh empire it winds its way further north over the dusty Punjab plains to Rawalpindi, on to Peshawar, gateway of the old North-West Frontier, over the Khyber Pass to Jalalabad and on to the Afghan capital, Kabul.

It measures out in millennia, miles and potholes the leaps of faith from Hinduism to Buddhism and Islam, the rise and fall of empires from the Persian, Mauryan, Mughal and British to today's independent India, Pakistan, and Bangladesh.

Epicurean adventurers are transported from Bengal's beloved shorshe maach (mustard fish) to the beef tikka kebabs of the frontier tribes, and the sartorial observer from the tartan wraparound lungis of the east to Punjabi 'westcots', Chitrali topis and Talibani turbans in the west.

Today it is just another part of India's National Highway network, but there is no better place to see what those civilizations have yielded and witness jugaad in all its definitions—frugal innovation, quick fix solutions bending the rules and beating the system, corruption—in action.

The family road trip watched over by Anand Mahindra in 2010 after our car's air conditioning broke down followed the ancient highway from Delhi to Chandigarh before turning right and heading north to the Kullu Valley at Nalagarh and it is a journey we've made most summers since we moved to Delhi in 2005.

It wasn't a smooth ride. We left our home in Delhi's B. K. Dutt Colony, a once Mughal Shia Muslim quarter and now a lower middle-class neighbourhood of two-room homes built by Hindu and Sikh refugees from Pakistan after Partition. We carefully passed our neighbours' scratched and dented rides to Jor Bagh Road, where cars from the posh colony opposite cut diagonally in front of us and a black and yellow autorickshaw headed us off on the inside. A cyclist riding one-handed while talking on a mobile phone drifted out obliviously from the left, forcing us to swerve right. We drove through Jor Bagh market, where an expensive SUV pulled out suddenly in front of us without indicating, forcing us to brake sharply, and then turned left into Lodi Road, past its gardens lined with tall palms and dotted with the ancient tombs of the Afghan Lodi emperors.

Motorcycles carrying families of five pulled away on amber, the youngest atop the petrol tank, siblings tucked between the father driving and the mother perched perilously yet gracefully side-saddle at the back. At the roundabout where Prithviraj Road meets the Taj Mahal Hotel, drivers sped on without checking for oncoming traffic and veered to edge us out of the way, while those wanting to exit to the left suddenly lurched across from the inner circle lane without indicating.

Some of the traffic lights were blinking red, amber and green in unison, cars, scooters, taxis and tempos were soon gridlocked and war declared for every inch or half-inch of tarmac. At other junctions, cars turning right took all three lanes, causing a long tailback of those heading straight on. Trees and monuments in the middle of the lane scattered drivers left and right, while elsewhere stray blocks of stone and mounds of sand sloped out into the road from unfinished or abandoned building works.

We rolled on the highway, cruised through Panipat's colour field of pickle shops, each hawking its famous pachranga five-colour condiment, stopped for an aloo paratha brunch at the Zhilmil Dhaba before heading on to Kurukshetra, scene of the Mahabharata's epic battle where Lord Krishna guided the good Pandavas to victory over their evil Kaurava cousins.

As we headed towards Ambala, we saw some overturned trucks and mangled cars. Unlicensed jugaad three wheelers, cobbled together from old scrapped parts of scooters, motorbikes, trucks and old tractors, passed us by.

Many of the truck drivers seemed tired. Some were hauling cement from the bleak factories of Bilaspur, just past Chandigarh on the climb up into the hills. Their drooping eyes reminded me of a taxi driver who once drove me from Jodhpur to Jaipur at five o'clock on a misty winter morning. I'd dozed off in the passenger seat but woke with a start to find the driver also snoozing and the bonnet of our car a good foot underneath the tail of a truck. When I yelled in terror, he opened his eyes, chuckled and said: 'No, no sir, you don't worry, sab theek hai.'

Just beyond Chandigarh, at the beginning of the climb up to Mandi, one of the oncoming, wildly weaving, trucks clipped our driver side wing mirror and took it clean off.

It was a lucky escape and reminder of a staple story in the Indian newspapers—the bus or truck which plunges over the edge of a mountain road or into a river below—local tragedies too small to be recorded beyond the domestic press, just more of those many que sera, chalta hai things.

Except, they're not cruel twists of kismet. Many of these instances are the predictable, preventable result of how people drive, the inhuman working conditions of truck drivers, the corner-cutting of their exploitative bosses, police corruption and an all-in, all-out war to beat the system, to win a race which cannot be won.

Our own victory was to reach Patlikul, crawl across the creaky suspension bridge over the raging Beas River at Pandara Mile, roll into the safe apple orchard haven of our cottage in cool, peaceful Batahar and collapse in relief that sixteen hours of National Highway driving was finally behind us. The honking horns of road rage had given way to birdsong, the chime of a temple bell and the faint drumbeat of a distant yatra somewhere on the other side of the valley.

The Grand Trunk Road we crossed and the mountain highway we climbed are among the world's most dangerous roads. More people die in road traffic accidents in India than in any other country in the world—137,572 were reported by the World Health Organization in 2015, almost 75,000 more than China which has a higher population.

The report noted that India has good laws which should reduce that number—good speed limits, laws against drunk-driving, and strict rules requiring drivers to use seatbelts and motorcyclists to wear crash helmets. But it also rated India's enforcement of these laws at between just two and three out of ten.

The fatal consequences of this state of affairs is no mystery to India's highway warriors. Mountain hairpins are marked with doggerel warnings daubed on rock faces: 'Caution and care make accidents rare', 'After Whisky, Driving Risky' and 'If You Love Her, Please Divorce Speed'.

Why do Indian drivers disobey traffic rules and why do the police officers who man the many checkpoints not enforce them adequately?

My Indian journalist colleague had given me a clue when he explained how driving licences are sold and that passing a driving test was more option than requirement.

It begged the question how many of India's drivers have actually passed a driving test or received a licence without paying a bribe?

According to Kiran K. Kapila, chairman of the Geneva-based International Roads Federation, the answer is way too few to hope for safer roads in the near future.

While there are reputable driving schools like those run by Maruti, the leading Indian car manufacturer, most are 'like shops', where the licence qualification is included in the course fee.

'They say we'll train you and get you the licence. There is no serious training effort on part of those small establishments...they have one or two vehicles which take you around a few times and then arrange to get you a licence in connivance with people who are not so honest... Many of the drivers are not adequately trained,' he explained.

India, he believes, needs more honest schools where drivers are properly trained, tutored in traffic rules and thoroughly examined and tested before being allowed to drive on the roads.

The first step would be to replace the old paper licences and require all drivers to take new, incorruptible tests before they receive new smart card versions, he explained.

Technology could help shunt corruption from India's roads. These smart cards would pave the way for a new instant fine or penalty points system which police officers could monitor though computer checks. Truck drivers falling asleep at the wheel could be monitored by sensors with 3G technology which beeps when the driver's eyes start to blink with fatigue and flicks on a siren if he doesn't stir, he suggested. Owners who illegally overload their trucks could be checked by police impounding their vehicles on the hard shoulder. They would be forced to send a rescue vehicle and another driver to transfer the load—extra expense as a penalty for infringement.

His proposals are premised on an honest police force, rather than one which demands weekly bribes from hauliers, taxi firms, street vendors and junction hawkers along with small 'chai-pani' bungs at mobile checkpoints.

My wife was asked for just such a bribe at a checkpoint just a few hundred metres from the prime minister's residence in the summer of 2014. The officer said the front bumper was obscuring the registration plate and produced a laminated rate card which indicated a fine of ₹1,000 for the infraction. When she asked for an official challan and said she would settle the fine at the court, the officer said it would save time if she simply gave him a few hundred rupees in cash.

Perhaps he hadn't been watching the news, or his seniors' demands for revenue had not yet been interrupted by the new order. Either way their brazen demand just a stone's throw from Prime Minister Modi's residence indicated the scale of the challenge facing him.

Kiran Kapila said technology could also be used to reduce police corruption.

Speed cameras could record infractions and policemen who then fail to issue a fine could later be questioned on suspicion of taking a bribe.

'This is what is the big problem [bribing]... So if I'm a police party standing at point X and it has allowed somebody whose number plate has already been read at higher speed and his challan has not been cut, then that policeman has to be questioned,' he explained.

I loved his optimism but realized my scepticism was bringing him down. I wound up the interview and decided to explore why, beyond the doggerel warnings, few drivers appeared to care about safety, why recklessness ruled the roads. I wanted to understand the thinking, the psychology of India's highway anarchy, and a diplomat friend told me about a Mumbai-based consulting company which might have some answers.

Final Mile Consulting is a rare and precious enterprise which finds solutions to some of India's seemingly intractable problems by studying the behaviour and concerns of the people causing them. They call themselves 'behaviour architects' and at the core of its work is a quest to understand why Indians behave and think the way they do by asking them.

Some of their projects have had spectacular results, like one in Mumbai where the authorities were alarmed at the number of people run over and killed by trains while crossing the city's train tracks. Final Mile's researchers discovered the poor who had to cross the tracks to go to work could not judge the speed of oncoming trains in the way they might a car because the railways do not have the signs and markers roads have to gauge distance.

So they installed a number of road-style markers at the worst black spots and soon found a dramatic decline in the numbers of people getting hit by trains. In some places deaths were reduced by 70 per cent.

The company has worked on other projects to find out why despite vast government spending on new toilets to stop open defecation many prefer to trudge to the fields—their new toilets are used as storage rooms instead.

But it was their research on the behaviour of truck and fleet car drivers that interested me most and I lured the company's founder Ram Prasad to tell me about their findings over a dram during one of his busy trips to Delhi.

Ram is a thickset Maharashtrian with an endearing line in self-deprecation who grew up in a village without electricity. He has a keen sense of the role scarcity and competition plays in Indian decision-making.

As a child he learned that the system was an obstacle to getting what you want or need and that bypassing official rules was the quickest and most efficient way to achieve your goals.

In a series of studies on why Indian drivers habitually break traffic rules, he found the same ideas at work.

In Delhi he interviewed a taxi driver who fixed a wide strip of black tape diagonally across his shirt each morning to fool distant policemen that he was wearing a seatbelt and not breaking the law.

Truck drivers told him how they rejected seatbelts because they fear being caught and lynched if they're involved in a road accident—they want to be able to make a quick getaway.

He interviewed fleet drivers for a foreign multinational who confessed that they observed the company's rule on keeping safe distances from other cars only while they were being watched—for fear of losing their jobs—but returned to breaking distances of just a few inches the moment they were out of sight.

'One phenomenon we see on Indian roads is people driving on the wrong side of the road. It's wrong, but the justification when you ask people is that the road is vacant, it's empty, and the right way means I must go 2 kilometres to make a U-turn. So what's wrong with what I'm doing? [They say] I do not have enough road on my side, or if I see an empty road I can drive wherever I want. I justify my driving on the wrong side of the road just because it's empty and because this process of going long and taking a U-turn is seen as naive so the jugaad is to drive on whichever part of the road is kind of empty,' he explained.

The drivers he interviewed and watched on simulators behaved as though they were involved in a race or competition and in situations where cooperation would have helped them achieve their goals or reach their destination faster or more safely.

The sudden lurching or cutting in front of another car, despite the risk of collision, or recklessly speeding onto a roundabout in front of cars with priority reflect a keenly felt instinct to 'win'. 'The scarcity we see on Indian roads is where there is this mad rush, even in bumper to bumper traffic, this "I want to be an inch ahead of the other person". Although it is not a competition in that way they see a competition in everything,' he said.

For truck drivers, many of whom are poor and of low caste or status, the road is the great leveller where their elevated position gives them the only competitive advantage they'll have in life.

'They are driving really long distances, crazy things are happening in their villages, someone's wife ran away, somebody had a child, they didn't go in time, they don't get too much respect in the village, but in the truck, you see, it's a release mechanism. I'm higher up, in a different hierarchy, therefore I drive differently. In the day you will see a lot of trucks speeding, a lot of brinkmanship really because you kind of assume yourself to be the truck, to be bigger, stronger, [a feeling] which otherwise does not exist in day to day life,' he said.

The excessive use of the horn reflects that race to win, to be the biggest and strongest on the road. When Final Mile tested drivers on simulators, they still honked furiously when a truck moved in front of them, even though they knew the situation was unreal and the truck driver on the simulator screen could not hear it.

The use of the horn is not simply a warning sound to alert other drivers to be aware of you passing, but an order to get out of the way, an assertion of might and the arrival of a fitter survivor.

'You think you control the road and the speed of the traffic when you honk, you think because you are honking things will change and we see a lot of that in India,' he said.

All of these behaviours, honking, speeding, road-hogging or straddling two lanes, cutting up other cars to get an inch or two ahead, they're all aspects of a cut-throat competition which is instilled in Indians from a very young age—all shortcuts, bypasses and jugaad ways to beat the system and win at all costs.

Indians grow up with this feeling from childhood, Ram Prasad said, that if they are not at the top of their game they will lose that dream job or college place to someone else. That if they are not first in line, someone else will take that coveted thing you want.

It is reflected in Indian film scenes, he said, where the tragic hero stands in line for a cinema ticket only to find the 'house full' sign when he finally gets to the front, or 'position filled' after queuing for a job interview.

For many Indians the scene is not just one of imagined pathos but a formative experience from their own childhood.

'As a child you want to go and watch a movie and you would see this board which says "House Full" because in a population of 100,000 maybe there's four or five movie theatres and that was the only form of entertainment. So, even though you've seen it once or twice it gets fixed in your memory, the fact that you went all the way, walking a kilometre or two to watch a movie and then there is this house full board.

'Or you're travelling by bus from one stop to another and there's this practice of people jumping on the bus through the window, throwing their handkerchiefs to signify reservation of seats, you see a lot of it,' he explained.

The expectation of scarcity is deeply ingrained. Too many people, not enough seats or jobs, and nobody wants to be that guy who gets there a few seconds too late.

The answer is to find your own way around the problem, contact someone you know who knows the box office manager or the ticket collector, make a deal with the bus conductor to keep your seats free.

'The idea of denial and scarcity where you have to go around to get something done is something that is in most Indians. You can't get things in a straight way, you have to go about it in a roundabout way. You have to be inventive rather than go through a defined process,' he explained.

In fact, the expectation of scarcity and the need to bypass the rules or beat the system is so ingrained that now when there is abundance in many areas of Indian life people artificially create shortages and people offer bribes to jump queues when they need not.

He cites the example of a recent trip to Zambia, when he needed a yellow fever vaccine, which is in plentiful supply but only available at one official vaccination centre close to Mumbai airport. Travellers must queue from 5 a.m. to stand a chance of getting their shots because the clinic will only give seventy per day. Once they have reached this number, those who missed out are accosted by middlemen to negotiate a price for getting the vaccine at an 'out of hours premium'.

When Ram Prasad told his friends, they weren't remotely surprised and one asked for the middleman's number because he would rather bribe than queue.

'The most interesting thing is when there is abundance, we are still creating scarcity so that we can create a subversion mechanism,' he said.

He had a similar experience when he tried to get his young son into a school where there were fifty applicants for each place. His friends were baffled when he insisted on following the normal selection process. They told him he was a fool, offered to help fix the selection through friends who knew the principal and accused him of naivety when he said he wanted to do it by the book.

Faced with a scarcity, people start looking for ways to bypass it rather than question the system that has led to the scarcity. 'In that case you either bribe someone or talk to someone who knows someone. The idea of raising something or having a fair discussion does not exist. You don't see cases of people raising [issues] with a cop or politician or government official, this kind of thing does not exist. So you are thinking the straight path is the difficult path, it's time consuming. The twisted path is easier,' he explained.

On the twisted path laws and regulations become guidelines or negotiable laminated rate cards, challenges to ingenuity or slipperiness. The road is neither black nor white but shades of haggled grey. Moral ideas of right and wrong or rights and duties are replaced by power and cash. But the possession of either, or even both, is no guarantee of victory or safety on the world's most dangerous roads as two tragic, unnecessary and contrasting deaths on the capital's streets in 2014 highlight.

Shortly after 6 a.m. on 3 June 2014, a few weeks after Narendra Modi won his historic election landslide, his rural affairs minister, the popular Maharashtrian farmers' leader Gopinath Munde, died following a collision.

He was en route to the airport in his white ministerial Maruti, complete with red flashing light to signal his VIP status, on his way home to celebrate his selection as a cabinet minister a week earlier. As his driver stopped at a junction on Delhi's Aurobindo Road, another car skipped the red light and crashed into his rear passenger door, seriously injuring his liver and causing other injuries which led to a fatal heart attack.

His death highlighted the lawlessness and poor governance

Mr Modi had been elected to tackle. The driver of the other car was arrested for causing the minister's death by dangerous driving and the incident brought calls for a review of road safety. Days later, Gopinath Munde's old BJP colleague, transport minister Nitin Gadkari, announced a meeting for all road safety stakeholders amid expectations of a review.

In it he made an unexpected announcement. The increasingly popular battery-powered rickshaws—the 'e-rickshaws' which had spread throughout the capital—would not be categorized as motor vehicles and their drivers could ply the roads without any training, qualification or licence.

Mr Gadkari also announced a government scheme to encourage their production because he believed they would benefit the poor.

His decision was hailed as a politically shrewd move which would win support among Delhi's estimated 80,000 e-rickshaw drivers, but it was strongly criticized by experts.

S. P. Singh of the Indian Foundation of Transport Research and Training told the *Times of India* that he was baffled at the move when the government had spoken of tightening road traffic rules after Mr Munde's death. More unregulated e-rickshaws posed a safety threat to their passengers and 'the common man,' he said.

On 29 July, around six weeks later, a young mother, Pinki Singh was carrying her two-and-a-half-year-old son Dev to Trilokpuri market in East Delhi when an e-rickshaw drove into her. She had planned to buy milk for her son and meet her husband Chhatar Singh, a poor daily wage labourer, and was walking on the road because local sweet shops had extended their operations onto the pavement to cope with increased demand during the Eid festival. When the e-rickshaw rammed into her, her infant was knocked from her arms and landed in a hot oil pan belonging to a sweet shop.

His mother reached into the vat to rescue him, severely burning her arms, and rushed him to hospital where he was pronounced dead a few hours later. The e-rickshaw driver abandoned his unstable vehicle and ran away, as did the sweet shop owner who had illegally used the pavement as his kitchen. The family was later given ₹1.1 lakh in compensation.

The police called for e-rickshaws to be banned and the High Court agreed, forcing thousands of the new vehicles off the streets. The government asked for them to be allowed to continue to ply their trade while they drafted new regulations, but the court rejected the suggestion.

Within a few weeks the minister yielded to the court, agreed to regulate e-rickshaws as a 'special category three-wheeled vehicle' and the ban was lifted. For the minister and Delhi's growing ranks of e-rickshaw drivers, normal business resumed.

Pinki Singh and her husband Chhatar, however, were left with their grief and ₹1.1 lakh in compensation.

CHAPTER 8

URBAN JUGAAD:
INDIA'S CITIES IN CRISIS

On 2 October 2014, Mahatma Gandhi's birthday, India's new prime minister Narendra Modi picked up a broom and swept the country into its most ambitious cleanliness drive.

The Swachh Bharat mission aims to achieve a 'Clean India' by the same day in 2019, the Mahatma's 150th birth anniversary. So, immediately after paying tribute to the Mahatma at his Raj Ghat memorial, the Prime Minister travelled to Delhi's Valmiki Sadan, where Gandhi regularly stayed among its 'untouchable' garbage workers, and began sweeping the street.

In his pristine white linen waistcoat and pale blue short-sleeved kurta, he pushed the broom before picking up leaves and litter and dropping them in a plastic bucket held by an aide.

The scene was captured by television crews and newspaper snappers: the most powerful leader India has seen in more than three decades getting his hands dirty and doing a job many higher caste Indians regard as the work of those whose very presence is pollution.

Some of his colleagues, however, were more concerned to be seen to be mucking in than making the city cleaner. At Delhi's Red Fort a few days earlier, reporters watched as garbage collectors were told to drop all their rubbish on the road outside so that the new culture and tourism minister could sweep it up for their cameras.

On the Hindon River, a tributary of the Yamuna just outside

Delhi, officials outsourced their planned sweep of its river banks to child labourers—ragpickers as young as eight. They were each paid ₹40 to trudge topless and barefoot through the river's toxic sludge and carry away hazardous waste while spotless officials were photographed in gloves and protective masks.

Despite the quick fix approach of some of his less-committed colleagues, Narendra Modi had made a bold start and he quickly roped in some of India's biggest actors, sporting heroes and business leaders to join him with their brooms. Master blaster cricket legend Sachin Tendulkar, Bollywood beauty Priyanka Chopra, billionaire businessman Anil Ambani and even the Prime Minister's Congress opponent, former External Affairs Minister Shashi Tharoor, accepted his challenge to roll up their sleeves and spread the message that public hygiene is a matter for all Indians, even, or especially, the rich, famous and high caste ones.

But if any of them had followed the adventures of 'The Ugly Indians', a clandestine group of volunteers and agent provocateurs who have spent the last six years reviving some of Bengaluru's worst garbage blackspots, they would have known there was much more to saving India's dirty, polluted cities than posing with the broom.

The Indian city is in crisis. Its multiplying residents are starved of electricity and water, public services are minimal or barely maintained, sewage floods their streets, pavements serve as rubbish dumps and public walls double as urinals.

Cities that should be celebrated for their history and architectural heritage are more often described as 'dirty, dangerous, unsightly, poor, disorganized, opportunist, corrupt, careless and inhumane,' said India's leading conservation architect Ratish Nanda to summarize the country's metropolitan anarchy.

The details of urban misery have become staple ingredients in the country's newspapers. Illegal and poorly constructed buildings collapse, roads subside and traffic is at a standstill. In the capital, unfit vehicles, battered buses and tilting trucks pump toxic fumes into the dusty atmosphere. In 2017, ten of the world's twenty most polluted cities were in India—Gwalior was branded the world's second most polluted city after Zabol in Iran, while Allahabad in Uttar Pradesh was ranked third. Delhi was the world's eleventh worst city for air quality. Bengaluru, India's 'garden city', 'Silicon Valley' and high-tech hope for the future, however, was not among them. The country's brightest software engineers work here for the world's biggest IT companies. The Indian Space Research Organisation, India's own NASA, has its headquarters here, along with the country's leading defence manufacturer, Hindustan Aeronautics Limited.

It is one of India's most cosmopolitan cities and on any given day its people are working on the next big smartphone app, tweaking a fighter jet or aiming a satellite at the Martian orbit.

But in October 2010, two of its inhabitants decided too many of their fellow Bengalureans were so focused on the heavens or the virtual world that they had overlooked the filth they were standing in. Only 2,100 of the 5,000 tonnes of rubbish generated by the city every day is collected by its waste management services. The remaining 2,900 tonnes is tipped into illegal dumps and thrown on the streets.

They posted a picture of one of these spots on their website along with a set of questions: 'Do you know this place? Is it like this because of corrupt politicians, lax municipal workers or because we don't care? Can we do something about it?'

The scene in the picture could have been snapped in any Indian city, but it was on Church Street, in the heart of Bengaluru's lively business and entertainment district. The pavement in front of a fenced-off electricity junction box had become an illegal rubbish dump. The fence and the pavement before it were broken and piled high with the trash of the surrounding offices, restaurants and fast food joints. There were plastic bags of every colour, coffee cups, polystyrene packaging panels and takeaway cartons with discarded snacks. A huge coil of cable had been abandoned there and a pedestrian was relieving himself on it.

Our sanitation spies watched the spot over seventy-two hours to establish exactly who was responsible for the mess and produced a forensic account of it on their site. Office workers from the *Times of India* building opposite and Wipro—one of India's leading technology companies—dumped their coffee cups and takeaway boxes there every morning while cleaners from nearby shops deposited their trash from the previous day.

The spot had once been home to a dumpster which was later removed in a state drive to make the city 'clean as Singapore'. Its then chief minister had believed that if he removed all the bins people would take their rubbish home and dispose of it in an eco-friendly way.

What in fact happens, our stake-out team discovered, is they simply dump it illegally in the same spots where the bins had once been, transforming them into filthy and smelly 'orphan sites'.

The site was also an underground intersection for storm water and sewage drains and, running through them, electricity and telecom cables belonging to the city's several broadband and telephone operators. At any given time, one of the seven or so government agencies or companies with subterranean hardware here is digging up the road or pavement to repair their cable or pipe below. The mud and stones they remove is left in a mound on the pavement and rarely put back—that's always somebody else's job.

When the sewage pipes became blocked and their contents flooded the ground above, government workers jumped in to remove the obstacles. Many of the area's power cuts, they explained, are caused by hungry rats which chew through the electric cables below these illegal city dumps. 'This is a great environment for wildlife, particularly rats, to breed, who feed on the garbage, gnaw on the electrical wires and eventually cause a short circuit and minor explosion and blackout. Very often, electricity blackouts are solved by removing the charred carcass of a rat from the wires,' one of our observers explained.

In fact, the illegal dumping site and rodent mela the site had become was considered an accepted part of the urban landscape and while no one liked it, no one saw it as their responsibility to clean it. And because it was a dirty dump, more people felt it was acceptable to toss their rubbish there: a classic example of what economists call a 'tragedy of the commons'.

But within three days our undercover heroes had changed the picture and posted the proof of what could be done if anyone cared enough: the rubbish was bagged and cleared, the pavement stones replaced and cemented, the cable coils and abandoned section of fence were removed and the curbstones painted black and white by turns. Potted plants were placed along the electricity junction box fence and the sidewalk was passable once again.

They called their intervention a 'spot-fix' and posted pictures of it on their website to inspire others to follow their lead. They had not blamed anyone for the mess, they had invited local security guards, sweepers, drivers and office workers to help them so all around felt like stakeholders, and it had cost them around ₹800. There had been no plenary sessions with experts, official no-objection certificates or self-congratulatory press conferences. It had been achieved by a couple of anonymous agent provocateurs with a few tins of paint, a bag of cement and the goodwill they'd created by asking local staff and workers for their advice and help.

Over steaming hot cups of chai at early morning tea stands, they'd formed friendships with the migrant guards, sweepers and cleaners many middle-class and high-caste Indians rarely regard, and then only as ancillary. Here, they were asking for their expert knowledge of the problem, enquiring about their own lives and offering to help them.

It was the start of a citizens' fightback not only against a 'helpless' or idle bureaucracy, official corruption and incompetent, uncoordinated government but also against deeply ingrained cultural habits. They had exposed one of the most visible and nocuous outcomes of jugaad quick fix thinking but refused to point the finger: it was every Indian's problem and theirs, exclusively, to solve. What was needed was a change of attitude and a few anonymous leaders. Anonymous because their selfless work must inspire rather than arouse suspicion of their motives. Their motto is 'Kaam chalu, mooh bandh'—'Just work, no talk': Their compatriots will talk and argue forever, they say, but rarely roll up their sleeves and get their hands dirty.

These particular Indians, however, are 'sick of waiting for someone else to do it for them. All the big talk of [Bengaluru] being a global city and all that is meaningless, if something like this can be allowed to happen right under your noses. And they have picked this spot as a symbol of all that is wrong. If they can reverse this civic disaster trend here, at this spot, they surmise, there is hope,' one of their collaborators wrote in an online book which records their experiment.

The book and website were provocatively named *The Ugly Indian* and blamed the squalor of the country's cities on widely shared cultural attitudes among its people.

'It's time we admitted that many of India's problems are because many of us are Ugly Indians. Look at any Indian street, we have pathetic civic standards. We tolerate an incredible amount of filth. This is not about money, know-how, or systems. This is about attitudes. About a rooted cultural behaviour. The Ugly Indian can take the world's best systems and find a way around it,' the protagonists explain on their site.

It could be a definition of jugaad—people bypassing systems, finding their own personal solutions which are often substandard or harmful to others.

I needed to talk to them, but they don't talk, they just work, and I couldn't fault them for that—I admire them.

After more than a year of emails and discussions on how we might talk without compromising their anonymity, I had given up hope of ever having a proper conversation with them.

But in early 2014, just as India's general election campaign got under way, an email offered a name—Anil Kumar—and a telephone number. It wasn't a real name but they had finally agreed to make a brief exception to their 'kaam chalu, mooh bandh' rule to explain their philosophy.

The group had read about a London Conservative councillor who was accused of prejudice in 2008 when she blamed Indian tenants for the state of the communal gardens surrounding their Hammersmith and Fulham flats.

'I know that in India throwing rubbish out of a window and total disregard for the cleanliness of a public area is normal behaviour and I dare say a number would change behaviour if firmly told that in London this is not acceptable behaviour,' she had said.

Her opponents seized on her statement and said she was wrong to single out Indians, forcing her to apologize for her 'ill-thought-out' and 'offensive' comments.

But according to 'Anil Kumar', the group's chosen spokesman, she was absolutely right and her story struck a chord with them: in neighbourhoods where 'Indians of Indian origin' are in a majority 'civic standards drop to Indian levels,' he said. 'Go to Little India in Singapore, huge fall in civic standards, or Southall [in London]… Because we are Ugly Indians we understand why we do what we do. There are certain reference points in your culture, many of the things non-Indians think are wrong, to Indians make tremendous sense,' he said.

It isn't a question of resources or systems, he explained, but of culture and religion. 'A Hindu is very inward looking. It is not about the priority of the commons. If you go to a mosque or church you will find that the commons are very clean, the commons and city centres. India is unique because of a particular religious cultural mix. [As Hindus] you look after your family first not your neighbour. Inward looking-ness and family unit makes it not normal to worry about the commons,' he said.

His group's mission is to lead a change in behaviour by using their own knowledge of Indian culture.

At one spot fix site the group carried out an experiment to see whether their grasp of Hindu cultural concerns could be deployed to deter public transgression. The site was an unloved sidewalk by a children's playground which had become a rubbish dump and open-air toilet. Volunteers cleared the rubbish, cleaned the pavement and then placed potted plants and painted blue hopscotch footprints on the stones. The message was that this was now a place people cared about and children played. For those who missed it, a stronger message was painted in a thick band of red—a sacred colour—along the wall.

The experiment was a success. The volunteers continued cleaning and extended the temple red band until all local offenders were corralled into one corner. They cleaned it up, installed a urinal and screened it from view.

Their approach combined a deep understanding of Indian jugaad thinking and cultural behaviour with a rigorous scientific approach of observation, interview and experimentation to lift people to higher civic standards.

Their urinals were illegal—the local authority had not been approached for permission—but because they worked, nobody objected. They were designed by a collaborator to be odour-free and cleaners were privately hired to maintain them.

Illegal dustbins were installed in breach of the city's then-existing no-bins policy and regularly cleared. They had learned that if bins are not regularly emptied, merchants destroy them to stop their shopfronts becoming a dump.

The bins themselves had to be redesigned to ensure everyone could use them. Removable bin lids are usually stolen—anything with a salvage value is pilfered, they found. Swing or swivel lids become a spittoon for paan chewers.

Their volunteers designed 'TereBins' to be too heavy to steal but narrow enough to stop dogs getting into them, and without lids which would become spit targets and deter others from using them.

As part of their research, our anonymous protagonists befriended the garbage truck driver who collected all the rubbish from the city centre and took it to a dump on the outskirts. He worked seven days a week and had to pay for truck repairs from his own pocket. When he reached the dump, he was occasionally stoned by locals who resented their village being commandeered without consultation to serve as a smoking waste site for the whole city.

The group's approach is to understand the causes behind the kind of behaviour that leads people to litter public spaces, and engage everyone in changing it without pointing the finger. Those who urinate in public do so because they have nowhere else to go. Even charity toilets charge a few rupees—the poor cannot waste six rupees per day when they can relieve themselves for free on any wall.

The garbage truck driver and the city road sweepers could be heroes if people valued their work, and even government officials who might benefit from the corruption are moved to help when they see people trying to improve their neighbourhoods, they found.

One solution is for residents to pay municipal sweepers a little extra to clean outside their homes, but many, including the wealthy, resent paying even a few rupees more when the taxes they pay for these services are diverted by corrupt officials.

The incentive can make all the difference to the poorly paid sweepers who are often cheated by employers who cut staff costs and share the windfall with officials. They have to clean more roads for the same money but cannot hope to meet their impossible targets. 'One woman has one kilometre of road to [sweep] per day. But whether it is residential or commercial the woman has much more to do because the government is cheating. She says if you pay me I will clean in front of your house. It used to be like that with the telephones and electricity. Everyone is looking out for themselves and it leads to a lot of heartburn. People won't pay on top because they're paying taxes. As a result, the whole system is broken. We deal with IT billionaires but when it comes to ₹11 a month it is a matter of principle! It breaks down on this issue, the lack of government and corruption,' Anil Kumar said.

What he and his co-conspirators have found in Bengaluru is a system that could eventually lead to a metropolitan public health crisis. It is the same in most Indian cities, but they are undaunted by it.

They believe they can change the Indian city by inspiring its people, and that its dysfunctional and corrupt systems can be subverted for the public good. Their lead has been followed in Mumbai where in 2017, volunteers led by a local environmentalist carried out what the United Nations called the 'world's largest beach clean-up project' at Versova, restoring what had become an illegal dump to white sands.

'It's jugaad because the government should be doing it but... we say just worry about your front and things will work themselves out. If you make it your problem to solve civic issues, you will get support as long as you don't ruffle feathers or interfere with the gravy train. We have never been stopped,' Anil Kumar explained.

In the meantime, the people of Delhi's growing megacity are fighting for every inch of its littered landscape.

Look closely in almost any direction across the urban vista and you will see something which is not supposed to be there. An istriwala doing the neighbourhood's ironing at a makeshift stand, often on the footpath, a rogue tea stand or a pavement barber lathering the whiskery chin of a customer perched on a pavement high chair facing a mirror nailed to a brick wall.

They are examples of what Kamal Nath, the veteran Congress leader and former minister for Urban Development, calls 'urban jugaad'—encroachment, the illegal construction or extension of homes, shops, residential colonies and jhuggi clusters on someone else's land.

Eighty per cent of Delhi's houses are believed to be illegally constructed without consent or in breach of building regulations, with occasionally catastrophic consequences. In June 2014, ten people were killed, including five children, when a house collapsed in East Delhi's Inderlok area. Investigators said illegal construction on either side of the building had been the cause.

As I wrote this, the steady, maddening thud of Kamal Nath's 'urban jugaad' was shaking my own house. In the narrow passage on our right flank two labourers were pile-driving into the foundations of the empty flat next door. My young designer neighbour Rakesh appeared on his roof to explain that they were inserting a reinforced steel beam to save the wall which supports his illegal duplex above the ground floor flat from collapsing.

It is a timely reminder of both the scale and peril of encroachment in the capital, an eternal stealth war fought by people to expand their footprint inch by inch.

I first noticed Rakesh's territorial ambitions a few years earlier when I heard a similar thumping noise. Labourers in flip-flops were smashing the top corner of a beautiful stone arch which linked our two buildings above the alley between.

Later, a blacksmith arrived and welded a steel staircase from the path up to the top of the arch to make a shortcut to the tenement's first floor balcony and the door to Rakesh's apartment. From the top of the new stairs, passers-by could peer into our then teenage daughter's bathroom.

No father would tolerate such an intrusion, and neither could I, or at least I didn't think I could.

I complained but my neighbour had invested too much in his campaign to care about my concerns. So I called the police and the New Delhi Municipal Corporation, and the illegal staircase was soon dismantled and abandoned on the path.

A week later, I heard the clang of sandal on metal and looked out to see the staircase had been wedged back into place, unwelded and precariously propped against Rakesh's first floor balcony. Stooped old ladies were clambering down it and every time they did, it looked like the staircase might collapse.

Their injuries would have been on my conscience so I gave up and put a heavy curtain over my daughter's window instead.

A few months later, two reinforced rolled steel joists (RSJ) appeared, poking out a few metres from Rakesh's flat towards our wall, serving notice that the shoogly stair was just one step on his social ladder. I couldn't tell exactly what he had in mind, but clearly it was a further expansion of his policies.

They had emerged a few days before we were about to head home to Scotland for our summer holiday and I forgot about them in the bustle of getting ready to go. When I returned a few weeks later, I noticed a bright light shining into our bedroom window overlooking the passage. The wall of Rakesh's flat, which had been a good 3 metres away, was now in touching distance. Its new coat of white paint was reflecting the bright street lamp into our room.

The RSJs had been an opening gambit, the first stage of a mid-air extension which had added a precious few extra feet to his living space. Another staircase connected his new first floor landing to the flat directly above, which I later learned he also owned.

New waste pipes had been fitted which now poured dirty water directly onto the path in front of my alley office—on bad days I would have to wade to work. When I asked him why he had not consulted me, he said: 'Because you would have complained!'

He had waged a patient campaign, adding to his property inch by inch until he had transformed it from a two-room symbol of lower-middle class hardship into a funky duplex with its own gated stair to the street below. Our young neighbourhood ironing man later told us Rakesh was hoping to get married and his new two-storey apartment was the key to marrying the girl of his dreams.

Now he's a catch, but only for as long as his ground-floor neighbour's wall bears the weight of his ambition. Today, his men are reinforcing the supporting wall to make sure it does.

I admired his fierce determination to improve his lot—especially if it was a love story too—and was grateful for the practical lesson in the mechanics of encroachment.

In fact, the more I looked, the more of it I noticed all around me. The makeshift covered stand, where our colony's istriwalas pressed the neighbourhood's clothes with charcoal-fired irons, is also an encroachment on the pavement. In the street opposite a barber has made a sidewalk salon with a stool, plastic mirror and rusty nail.

At the gate to the nearby Lodi Gardens park, a young man picks green coconuts from his battered hatchback and hacks them open on the pavement for thirsty walkers under the fierce gaze of a khaki-clad police officer.

The cop watches his unlicenced trade to make sure he and his fellow officers receive the correct amount in kickbacks: a weekly hafta of ₹4,000 for the pitch. He must sell more than a hundred coconuts before he starts making any money for himself but if sales increase, the men in khaki will want more, the young man explained.

The pavement jalebiwalas, fast-food joints, alfresco barbers, neighbourhood ironing stands, fruit and vegetable stalls are all unlicenced and illegal but their encroachment is overlooked by those responsible for enforcing the law in exchange for a weekly 'rent'.

And unless their encroachment impinges directly on someone else's private property, few object. Their services are mostly wanted and the only space available for them is on government-owned public property for which Delhi Police has appointed itself commercial landlord. It is a jugaad solution to low police pay and the scarcity of land which has robbed the capital of much of its sidewalk space and even cut into the roads.

My favourite jugaad encroachment was an act of divine inspiration. Nizamuddin basti, home to one of the most revered Sufi shrines, is also a Mecca for kebab lovers who park their cars outside Aap Ke Khatir (Your Pleasure) takeaway and its neighbouring rival Sab Ke Khatir (Everyone's Pleasure) and slow the traffic to a halt.

The sidewalk kebab stands and their plastic tables and chairs are an illegal annexation of public land and when the Municipal Corporation decided to reclaim it, the owners came up with a further encroachment to safeguard the first. Nizamuddin is an urban village built around the graves of Muslims who wanted an auspicious burial close to the shrine of the saint who gave the area its name. Destroying a grave or shrine is considered unacceptable in India since that would mean disrespect to religious beliefs.

One night, the kebabchis told me, shortly before the demolition men arrived to destroy their businesses, a new, brightly tiled 'ancient' Islamic tomb 'suddenly appeared' in front of the kebab stands to settle the matter. Today, there is no more talk of demolition and the kebabchis continue to do a roaring trade.

The reality of the Indian city is that there are too many people but not enough land. Few have the space they need or the money required to buy it, so they take what they can, bit by bit, until council officials or police officers notice and an arrangement can be made.

Even when new housing settlements are built to give legal status to poor squatters and slum-dwellers living on the margins, extreme hardship and bad policies soon drag the beneficiaries back into the twilight zone.

In her study, *Tolerated Encroachment*, Ursula Rao documented the progress of squatters who were resettled in West Delhi's Savda Ghevra colony between 2008 and 2010. They were offered 18 square metres of land on a ten-year lease for ₹7,000 on the condition that they built a home within three months. The leases could not be sold or traded.

But within months several of the new residents had illegally handed over their original leases to moneylenders as collateral for loans to build their new homes. One poor family officially owned two tiny resettlement plots but had sold one and mortgaged the other and no longer had documents to prove ownership of either. Their buyer and lenders had the title deeds to plots they were not allowed to own.

The same patterns of encroachment and illegal occupation of land which characterized life in middle-class neighbourhoods appeared to be mirrored among the poorer and more marginalized communities too. The difference was one of scale.

A few streets away from B. K. Dutt Colony, India's senior civil servants and powerful politicians have built unauthorized extensions and made illegal changes to some of the country's most coveted homes—the government-owned whitewashed bungalows which line New Delhi's wide avenues.

According to Malvika Singh, publisher of *Seminar* magazine and a leading conservationist, government secretaries, members of parliament and ministers are guilty of some of the capital's worst encroachment offences.

She feels proprietorial about the capital's architectural heritage—her husband's grandfather, Sir Sobha Singh, was one of Sir Edwin Lutyens's main collaborators and built some of New Delhi's most important colonial buildings, including Rashtrapati Bhavan, India Gate and most of Connaught Place.

The new capital of British India was conceived as a showcase for colonial planning with strong influences from the subcontinent's own history.

It was a garden city, as was Shahjahanabad, Delhi's old Walled City, which was built by the great Mughal emperor on a grid system with tree-lined avenues and cooling water channels. Like Jaipur, built by Maharaja Jai Singh in the eighteenth century, New Delhi's boulevards and circuses had geometry.

Its whitewashed bungalows, set on wide green lawns, had high ceilings with fans to circulate cooling air, verandas for senior officials to relax in, fireplaces to heat the grand rooms in harsh Delhi winters, and bright terrazzo floors—chips of coloured marble set in emerald, dusty pink or cobalt cement—which sparkle in the light.

They are as highly coveted today by political leaders, generals, judges and senior civil servants as they were in the last days of the raj.

But according to Malvika Singh, their new custodians have destroyed much of the original charm with jugaad extensions and modifications.

'We have a lot of people on the bench, government employees... they feel the laws made for me can be broken by them, it has destroyed this city,' she said, in *Seminar's* Connaught Place salon office.

She said she could think of only three senior politicians who had restored their bungalows in accordance with their original plans. 'Everyone else has added, enclosed verandas inside the building, bedrooms, ripped out the terrazzo floors because they think bathroom tiles are more pleasing...they have all done things like put rooms on the second floor, [used] hideous asbestos sheets, because the law says if there are no foundations it is not an encroachment. Cabinet ministers, they have all added portacabins saying they need extra space for PAs, or 90 per cent have rented out their servants' quarters to people who don't serve them and are making illegal money from rent. Secretaries to the Government of India, many of them rent out servants' quarters to tailors, carpenters and get their work for free, clothes stitched. They are exploiting the place, changing the windows, breaking down walls. The whole construct of the city as planned gets mutilated within the walls of the house,' she explained.

She and her husband Tejbir Singh live in Sujan Singh Park, an Indo-Edwardian redbrick apartment block built around the art deco Ambassador Hotel in 1945 to house the vast extended family of his grandfather, Sir Sobha Singh. Its flats are still mostly occupied by relatives who pay peppercorn rents to a family trust which requires them to retain their original features.

The Singhs are devoted to conservation, but scathing of local government officials who watch for minor infractions to solicit bribes while nearby the political elite is destroying the capital's Lutyens heritage.

When Malvika's son rebuilt a damaged wall outside his flat, officials quickly arrived to say it was illegal and to solicit bribes. 'I said if you try anything with me you will be in the cooler,' she said.

It's a threat few would take lightly. Malvika, or Mala as she is known, is a force of nature, the daughter of the late left-wing firebrand Romesh Thapar, niece of India's most celebrated historian Romila Thapar, and daughter-in-law of the family which laid the ground most Dilliwalas walk on. When the illegal newspaper sellers, who lay out their journals on the pavements of Connaught Place are being chased by the police for higher hafta payments, they hide in her office.

For her, the encroachment of pavements, construction of illegal, substandard buildings and the threat to the city's unique architectural heritage are all of a piece.

Officials join the government's Urban Development Ministry or the municipal corporation not because they are passionate about city planning or architecture but because it is 'a money-making racket' in which wealthy property developers pay them to look the other way. 'In that context of haphazard city growth on the whim of the builder, the builder says we will give you a family flat somewhere for giving me a no objection [certificate]. The real action is in real estate,' she explained.

Until Narendra Modi's BJP swept to its landslide victory in the 2014 election, Kamal Nath was India's urban development minister, the man charged with bringing order to this 'haphazard growth' and the daunting task of reviving the Indian city.

A stalwart of the Congress Party, he was probably the best hope that government had. The irony of his appointment was that a man who had earlier held a favourable view of jugaad was now the man in charge of clearing up the urban mess it had created.

In 2007, as India's commerce and industry minister, he paid tribute to the nation's jugaad spirit in his book, *India's Century*. Jugaad, he said, described the 'ability to creatively "manage", to make do with quick-fix solutions' and it had become 'a survival skill for most Indians. It was the additional resource that gave greater returns within a framework of scarcity' and its use turned every obstacle into an opportunity.

Then he wondered if jugaad represented a 'suppressed Indian inventive gene' which had led its early scientists to discover the concept of zero and the value of pi in mathematics more than 2,000 years earlier.

But as urban development minister in 2011, he found the 'inventive gene' being put to more ignoble causes.

India's cities had been overrun by refugees from Partition and the Bangladesh war, and then again by ever-increasing waves of migrants from rural India.

The human tide became a 'tsunami', he said, and the sprawling metropolises that emerged were left with severe shortages of housing, electricity, water and sanitation. 'Growth has preceded environment in urbanization, it has preceded infrastructure. leading to urban jugaad,' he said.

'Urban jugaad means somebody sets up at the back of a house, an encroachment: it is jugaad. It is this economy of shortages,' he explained.

The scale of his task and the paucity of resources for him to tackle it stopped him in his tracks. 'I do not know where to start, I open it and I'm dead because there is such a huge deficit in urban infrastructure,' he confessed.

The city is under siege not only from young migrants from rural India and lawless encroachment, but also from an 'overdose of democracy' in which vital new roads and other essential services are stalled by perpetual legal challenges.

'Somebody was telling me when I was transport minister that 50 kilometres [of new roads] means 50 court cases,' he said.

New Delhi was built as symbol of British colonial power and planning between 1911 and 1931, but in a 2017 Urban Development Ministry survey, Delhi was ranked only as India's seventh cleanest city. Indore topped the list and Mumbai, India's greatest megacity, scraped in at number 29.

Chandigarh, Nehru's modernist ideal for independent India, has been recognized as India's cleanest, wealthiest and most developed city at various times over the last eight years, but it too is showing signs of wear and tear.

The concrete city built in the early 1950s by the Swiss-French architect Le Corbusier as a modernist post-Partition replacement for Lahore, was created as an expandable city of wide-avenued sectors which could be replicated by its planners as its population grew. It stood in stark contrast to Lahore and Delhi's walled cities where brick buildings huddled together to cast cooling shadows over the narrow alleys and people below. Chandigarh was a statement that an independent India could escape its past and embrace its own modern future.

But however much Nehru had wanted the city to herald a new Indian future, it gradually yielded to the wider culture and past it had risen from. Over time it steadily came to resemble the older

Indian cities it was designed to succeed.

I visited the city during the chaotic and hard fought general election campaign of 2014. Everywhere I went during my visit a large majority of the people I spoke to expressed widespread anger, frustration and unhappiness over the immense amount of corruption to be found in their city as well as the squalid living conditions of Chandigarh's largest vote bank—the poor servants, labourers, rickshaw drivers and various other sections of the poorest segments of society who live in the slums.

The contest pitted the glamorous actress Gul Panag, who campaigned for the anti-corruption Aam Aadmi Party astride an Enfield Bullet motorbike, against film and television actress Kirron Kher of Narendra Modi's BJP.

At a hustings held by public sector workers in a run-down community hall, they heard how officials were stealing staff salaries to line their pockets.

'If I am a [government] contractor paid to hire fifty workers, instead I will employ ten and the wages of the forty others will be divided between the contractor and the government officer. The workers will get less,' Bhupinder Singh Gill of the Federation of UT Employees and Workers Chandigarh, explained.

The candidates heard how the city's legion of pensioners had to pay bribes to collect their benefits or even to pay electricity bills without queuing for hours.

In Daria on the southern city limit, where the winner was expected to be decided, the wide boulevards of Chandigarh gave way to bumpy mud tracks flooded with raw sewage.

The economic history of independent India has been measured out in Moscow-style five-year plans which span the socialist focus on heavy industry and infrastructure—dams and steel plants—under Nehru and the economic liberalization guided by Dr Manmohan Singh in 1991 and continued under Narendra Modi until 2017.

Why had a country which had invested so much in the idea of planning after independence planned so poorly?

For Kamal Nath, shortly before he was ousted from office by Narendra Modi's landslide victory, the answer was in something akin to lip service. Indian governments and prime ministers had talked much about planning but never invested in the people and skills to put ideas into action.

'We don't have trained people. My biggest challenge in urbanization in this ministry and in the states is capacity building. I don't have trained people, there is no municipal cadre. We never set up these institutes to train town planners, any planning people, we're now going about doing it. Nobody expected urbanization to happen at such a pace,' he explained.

The infrastructure deficit is so great, he said, that 'what we do in the next ten years will not be building for the future, we'll be catching up with the past.'

His stark outline is a common reason why many of the country's captains of industry have backed the creation of 'Special Economic Zones'.

The idea was explained to me by Mukesh Ambani, India's wealthiest tycoon, in an interview for the *Sunday Times* in 2006. India had the young talent to flourish in the increasingly globalized economy, but its cities do not have the infrastructure. If companies like his Reliance were to invest in new cities of five million people, build new power stations, roads, railways, homes and first-class schools and hospitals, then the world's best brands could be attracted to manufacture their wares in India. The best Indian talent which now seeks opportunities overseas could be lured home by a lifestyle hitherto unavailable in India.

Unlike in India's grubby real cities, where corrupt politicians and civil servants can hold hopes of progress and development to ransom, in SEZville the corporate owner would be the planning regulator, the healthcare provider and the education authority. The insurmountable obstacles which prevent existing Indian cities becoming modern or world class could simply be brushed aside—a jugaad solution to the urban jugaad which daunted Kamal Nath.

Mukesh Ambani's plan was to invest $11 billion in two new cities, one in Mumbai, the other near Delhi, to house five million people in each.

'In India, what do we have? A large amount of talent. Our biggest challenge is to grow with globalization. We have twenty million young people coming into the workforce every year. We have people, goods and services. What we do not have is integrated infrastructure. The model I am creating is employment-led. If we can create five million jobs over the next five years giving $5,000 per capita where the world would pay $15,000, then we give the employer a $10,000 advantage,' he explained.

'Can we supply the power and infrastructure to create goods and financial services? When we can say that we can, we will be able to attract Nike to make shoes, or Sony and Samsung to make television sets. We believe we can create a quality of life where our brightest people do not have to go to Britain and America.'

He was inspired by Shenzhen, the SEZ close to Guangzhou in Southern China, which grew to become a megacity in its own right by attracting the world's biggest manufacturers.

India's soaring population—it is expected to overtake China's by 2024—gives it a democratic advantage over its regional rival, he explained.

'It will become old before it becomes rich. India will get rich before it gets old,' he said.

Ten years on, the Special Economic Zones Mukesh Ambani and other Indian tycoons had banked on have yet to rise from the plans while India's old megacities have grown bigger and more congested. According to UN estimates their growth will continue to accelerate—Delhi's 23.5 million population will increase to 36 million by 2030.

The comparison Mukesh Ambani drew with China raises niggling and persistent questions for India. How has India's regional rival succeeded in building vast modern metropolises while India's cities have plunged so deep into an environmental abyss that the Prime

Minister himself is wielding the broom?

The aspiration to rival China is felt keenly in India, especially by the older generation which remembers its humiliating defeat in the 1962 war over their disputed Himalayan border.

After China embraced economic liberalization under Deng Xiaoping in 1979 it invested heavily in major infrastructure projects—highways, dams and modern cities. When I first visited the country in autumn 1988, the cranes had only recently appeared on Shanghai's horizon to build Pudong. Today it is a skyscraper metropolis in its own right with a population of more than five million people.

It is a triumph of Chinese planning and management systems and the closest comparison India can draw is with Gurgaon, Delhi's satellite city just over the state border in Haryana which is home to several Indian and multinational offices, manufacturing plants, tech companies, start-ups and BPOs.

The land for Gurgaon was acquired and developed in a bold, innovative scheme by a small number of Indian real estate entrepreneurs, including former cavalry officer K. P. Singh. He bought plots of land from small farmers and then persuaded them to plough their windfall into his vision of a new, modern city on the edge of India's capital. It made him one of the world's wealthiest billionaires.

Gurgaon rose in part from his extraordinary salesmanship and looked to the outsider, at first glance, like a modern Western or Southeast Asian business district— an Indian Singapore.

When we moved to Delhi in 2005, it had a near monopoly of air-conditioned shopping malls, cinemas and Western restaurant chains and quickly became our family's Sunday refuge from the summer heat.

Some friends suggested we should make our home there. Its modern high-rise apartment blocks had spacious flats with guaranteed twenty-four-hour water and power—unique in Delhi, even in the Lutyens Bungalow Zone where the country's cosseted leaders are shielded from the reality of their own stewardship.

Its 'modernity' however gives way to a more traditional Indian urban landscape when you lower your gaze from the glass and steel above to chaos below.

Even today, few of its buildings have pucca link roads to connect them to Gurgaon's main boulevards. Their surrounding grounds have not been landscaped but left as foraging scrub for drifts of wild pigs. Despite the presence of some of the world's largest and wealthiest companies, the roads are cratered with potholes. Gap sites between developments have become stagnant waste water ponds.

In some developments, builders have failed to ensure adequate water supplies or sewage services. At one prime site, the colony's sludge is illegally pumped by an old tractor engine up to the surface and then through a thick pipe into the municipal sewer.

Gurgaon is the fact which contradicts those who claim that India's urban jugaad and chaos is explained by the 'human tsunami' which submerged its cities, that migration overtook planning and infrastructure development—that India simply has too many people to be planned. The new 'smart city' has seen a rise in migrants—many of them construction workers building its gleaming tower blocks—but not on the same scale as Delhi. Yet all the hallmarks of Indian city chaos are there in abundance all the same.

How had the modern 'miracle' of Gurgaon descended into traditional urban anarchy?

According to two Indian civil servants known for their probity, corruption is the root cause of the malaise. They allege that many of the plots sold to developers are reassigned from agricultural to commercial land not as a result of public interest planning or civic ambition but illegally and as a result of corruption.

One of them, Ashok Khemka, provoked a national outcry in 2012 when he alleged irregularities in land deals involving Congress president Sonia Gandhi's son-in-law, Robert Vadra. The IAS officer was charge-sheeted by the Congress government in the state for exceeding his jurisdiction in the matter (the charge-sheet was subsequently revoked by the successor BJP regime which came to power in Haryana in 2014). Khemka was later transferred from his post—his forty-third transfer in twenty years. Mr Vadra strongly denied any wrongdoing.

Mr Khemka's treatment was by no means unique. His IAS colleague Pradeep Kasni was also transferred from his post after he submitted a report that revealed how government officials were colluding with land grabbers in 2014. He called for an investigation into the officials who had approved the deal but instead he was disciplined. By the time he retired in February 2018, the officer had been transferred seventy-one times in a career spanning thirty-four years.

His reputation for honesty had blighted his career and it grew after he refused a briefcase full of cash for obliging a personal request in one of his earliest postings. 'I had already said yes but it was the giving of money, as if he had bought me, that was intolerable,' he explained.

For him it was a question of self-respect, but it marked him out as a threat to some other civil servants who had deemed it better to compromise with the system. When I met him in his Chandigarh office, he quoted a couplet he attributed to India's former prime minister V. P. Singh, who was known for his plain dealing: 'Who are you to buy me? I'm free.' His family has paid a high price for his honesty. His children's education was disrupted by more than twenty house moves. 'It's a miniscule percentage that are honest—you can count them on your hand. It is impossible to prosper,' he said.

His colleague Dr Satbir Singh Kadian said their penchant for probity had left these officers isolated within their service because few colleagues talked to them. 'Who will Pradeep Kasni talk to? He comes to me, I go to him, he goes to Khemka. Who will we sit with?' he asked.

Widespread corruption reflects the primacy of private interest over civic concerns in the growth of India's cities but it cannot entirely explain the public squalor. China, which has well-planned cities and high-quality infrastructure, is ranked level with India in Transparency International's Corruption Perceptions Index, 2015, while corruption in well-developed Thailand is worse.

Why have India's leaders and people not been able to develop and maintain modern cities like China? Both countries emerged as new states amid great upheaval at around the same time. Mao Zedong declared his People's Republic of China in 1949 from the rubble left by years of Japanese military occupation and civil war. Independent India suffered the largest mass migration in history following the partition of 1947. Yet from comparable chaos and hardship—for Punjab and Bengal in any case—it was China that built the better cities.

Malaysia and Singapore, which endured British colonial rule for longer than India—they did not become independent until the early and mid-1960s and were affected by a Communist insurgency for much of the decade—have created world class cities and in many respects outstripped their old imperial ruler.

Why not India?

The comfort answer for Indian politicians and opinion formers is to blame its chaos on the burden of being the world's largest democracy. Its 1.3 billion people are free, assertive and would not yield to the authoritarian approach of Singapore or Malaysia, let alone the diktat of Chinese government. India's urban squalor and pandemonium are badges of freedom, they suggest.

By chance one of the key urban planners behind the rise of Singapore and the architect of many Chinese cities, happened to be in India and considering the same question, just as I was struggling with it.

Liu Thai Ker helped oversee the development of Singapore from the poverty of its early years of independence to its place today as the world's third wealthiest country.

Between 1969 and 1989, he was architect-planner and chief executive of Singapore's Housing and Development Board which oversaw the creation of more than twenty new towns of 200,000 people to rehouse those who had languished in squatter camps.

He went on to plan more than a dozen cities of up to

five million people in China, including Xiamen, the ancient southern port city of Amoy. It is today considered one of the country's best cities to live in.

Having been at the heart of Singapore's renaissance in the 1960s and a key figure in fast-tracking urban development in China, he is uniquely placed to explain how drowning cities can be rescued and why India's conurbations are going under.

In its first years of independence, he said, Singapore shared the sanitation and overcrowding problems which submerge Delhi, Mumbai and other Indian cities today. In 1960, two-thirds of its 1.9 million people lived in squatter camps and its rivers were toxic and regularly flooded the city's roads.

'Singapore was not dissimilar to Old Delhi. Hard to imagine but it was dirty, smelly, the river was sulphuric, just a sewer. That's what I remember when I was a kid,' he recalled. 'It was marginally better than Delhi but no sewers, water was from common pipes.'

The new state's visionary but authoritarian leader Lee Kwan Yew banked on planning to raise his city from the sludge to one which could attract foreign investors.

He 'greened' the city with trees, created a modern sewage system and built new homes to tackle the chronic housing shortage.

He picked a few low-cost projects 'to send a message to citizens and government officials that there is hope for your city and pride you can take in your city. Do something to stimulate hope and possibility,' he said.

Outline plans grew from assessments of what kinds of roads it would need, how many schools, homes, parks and commercial centres. 'A city is a machine for living,' Liu explained. 'These are the spare parts of the machine. If a planner does not know which spare parts need to go into a city how can he plan it well?'

China's socialist system made it easier for officials to acquire and earmark land—the basic unit of development—for infrastructure projects, he said. But its main advantage over India was in its commitment to development.

'My sense is that they're totally clear that they must be development-orientated. There is a hesitance about it in India. The opposite side of China is India,' he said.

He had given a talk in India on how to build cities and was surprised when the organizers asked him how they could convince their state's chief minister about the value of planning and development.

'"We have a serious uphill battle," they said...the government agenda is not that clearly development-orientated. Probably more problem-solving, whereas China wants to go beyond that and improve its economy. In China it's a management system and the goals are clearer,' he said.

India is so far behind China and Singapore that drawing up a comprehensive development plan would have little meaning. Its first task is to break through urban despair and create a few showcase sites to offer a glimpse of hope and something people can be proud of.

'The highest priority is to improve the sanitary aspect and give people a sense of pride. At the moment there is no sense of pride,' he said.

CHAPTER 9

YATRA'S END:
A T-POINT ON JUGAAD MARG

Barely eighteen months after the euphoric success of the *Mangalyaan* mission to Mars and the triumphant launch of jugaad innovation into outer space, Narendra Modi was brought crashing down to earth.

The Prime Minister had been in Mumbai to promote Make in India—his flagship policy to encourage local and international companies to build factories and bring new technology, jobs and wealth to India. Delegates from more than fifty countries attended the event which was to culminate in a Chowpatty Beach dance extravaganza featuring some of Bollywood's biggest stars.

Despite Modi's long association with Hindu nationalism, his landslide victory in the 2014 election was widely regarded as a vote for development, to replicate the economic success he'd presided over in Gujarat throughout India.

India's most pressing need is jobs. According to official figures more than a million young people enter the labour market every month but the Indian economy doesn't have the jobs to employ them. Between 1991 and 2013 its working age population increased to 300 million but only 140 million found work.

Modi's task is to create at least a million new jobs every month and for that he needs the world to see the true potential of a country that can put an underpowered rocket into the orbit of Mars for less than the cost of a Hollywood studio movie.

Mangalyaan was Modi's 'Man on the Moon' Kennedy moment when frugal rocket science and jugaad thinking converged to discover a new frontier of possibility. Its success offered a different narrative to tempt investors but as the country's leading Bollywood stars shimmied on stage, a darker kind of jugaad threatened to cloud his vision in thick black smoke.

As leading actor Aamir Khan looked on and organizers urged Amitabh Bachchan, Bollywood's biggest star, back into the spotlight, an 'angry orange spark' lit the 'decorative foliage' and within minutes Mumbai's Make in India promotion went up in flames.

Had Bachchan returned to the stage, he might not have lived to count his blessings. India's reputation as an investment destination, however, suffered severe burns. An event to promote Indian capability had highlighted the continuing threat of corner-cutting and quick-fix thinking.

A Fire Investigation Report found a defective electrical circuit and organizers' failure to follow safety rules had sparked and fanned the flames. They had wanted to create a visual spectacle of fire passing through a tubular idol of Lord Ganesha, remover of obstacles and God of new beginnings, and ignored repeated instructions not to use Liquefied Petroleum Gas to create the effect.

In the space of a few days, potential investors from around the world were not only shown the range of skills India offers but also treated to a live horror show highlighting the real risks of doing business there.

In just eighteen months, Modi had experienced both the cosmos conquering combination of Indian science and good jugaad thinking and the excruciating embarrassment of its quick-fix corollary. He too had walked our yatra.

◆

Our journey began with the best of frugal jugaad innovation in the work of home inventors like octogenarian M. B. Lal whose Snowbreeze air conditioner offers affordable cooling to India's poor;

Dharamveer Kamboj, a former rickshaw puller whose fruit-pulping machine not only made his fortune but transformed those of his fellow villagers too; and Amrutbhai, the former child labourer whose farm inventions not only save backbreaking labour but lives too.

The jugaad approach to problem solving has created the world's cheapest car, brought clean drinking water and affordable surgery to poorer families.

We've heard from some of the world's wealthiest business tycoons who attribute their vast fortunes to a quick-fix approach to deal making—jugaadism, as Gopichand Hinduja calls it. For them it's a willingness to think laterally and embrace unconventional thinking.

We have witnessed the destructive power of jugaad too on India's urban and natural landscapes from the unplanned construction chaos and overwhelmed infrastructure of its cities to the killing of its rivers by toxic chemicals and sewage.

We've studied jugaad in business, politics, medicine, education and manufacturing. And we've looked at the role of jugaad decision-making on the roads and in hospitals.

The best jugaad has a measure of altruism or community purpose behind its frugal and hand-made solutions, the worst can embrace the reckless, venal and deadly.

One side has a strong can-do optimism, the other a self-serving cynicism.

What they share is the work of resourceful individuals with a unique genius for circumvention—working around problems and dealing with their effects rather than confronting the causes head on.

Early in our journey we heard how the post-independence years were an era of hardship and scarcity in which necessity was the mother of invention and jugaad thinking an essential survival tool.

The 70th of independence in 2017 offered a moment to look back not only at the sacrifices made in its march to freedom and the pain of Partition but also the resilience and innovation which flourished as people found new ways to survive and prosper in the face of poverty, overcrowding and corruption. For many the jugaad solutions which saw people through those years of scarcity and hardship are a source of enduring pride.

Inevitably, the anniversary also raised questions about India's future. How will it fare in its next seventy years? How can it match or overtake the development of the world's leading economies? For some the answer to this question lies in the role jugaad thinking plays in it—whether it is embraced as a low cost USP or banished as an obstacle to progress. What role can or should jugaad play as India seeks to tackle the world's greatest socio-economic and political challenges over in the decades ahead?

By 2024, India's population will reach 1.4 billion to surpass China as the world's most populous nation. By 2050, its population is expected to reach 1.66 billion.

Its stressed, polluted and overpopulated major cities are forecast to grow by between 6 and 8 per cent by 2021—Delhi is already the world's second largest metropolis and by 2030, its numbers will have increased from twenty-six to thirty-six million. They will need more homes, power, water, schools, hospitals, cars, trains, buses, motorbikes, sewage and waste disposal systems and it will take every percentage of economic growth and all the problem-solving creativity it has to deliver them.

India's leading thinkers are fiercely divided on what role, if any, jugaad thinking can play in building its future. Some believe inspired circumvention will be essential if the country has a hope of meeting the surge in need it faces while others believe jugaad will only sabotage its prospects of meeting it.

Environmentalist Sunita Narain said India simply cannot afford the expensive Western-style big infrastructure investment it would need to stop its cities from drowning in their own waste. It will never be able to fund the vast number of sewage treatment plants and pipe systems it needs or install toilets and connect the soaring population of urban poor to the network. It can't even afford the electricity to keep its existing water treatment plants operating.

'We create the hardware, we design a cleaning up programme,

a blueprint from somewhere else in the world and then we try to fit it into our situation where it completely falls apart,' she said.

The answer, she said, doesn't lie in big-system solutions, but in small scale, Indian jugaad.

She offers her Centre for Science and Environment in Delhi as a small-scale alternative—it harvests rain, composts waste and recycles all its water to be self-sufficient. She would like to see similar local initiatives in every city and every building, but India is too enamoured with Western infrastructure systems to think differently. 'I don't think we respect the jugaad way,' she said. 'We are very fascinated by ways that were adopted by the rest of the world and we think we will be able to find the same solution... It is a pipe dream.'

Industrialist Anand Mahindra rejects the idea that jugaad can have any part in India's future but he shares Sunita Narain's view that many of the answers lie in small scale solutions. He doesn't accept her description of it as a jugaad approach but echoes her argument that great progress can be made without necessarily tackling the country's failing systems head-on.

He calls it a 'distributed' or 'off-grid' solution that offers new technologies to empower people now rather than wait for wider system solutions that could take forever.

He cites the provision of clean drinking water as an example. Only seven of India's twenty-nine states and seven union territories provide potable water to their villages. In cities and villages throughout the rest of the country the groundwater is polluted with toxic chemicals and many children under five die from water-related diseases.

How long will people in those other states wait for safe water? He supports the work of the NGO Naandi which sets up small water treatment plants and sells clean drinking water to villagers for ten to twenty paise per litre.

So far Naandi has established more than 400 treatment plants to provide three million people with safe water. Could it be a solution for the whole country?

'To me that is the answer, a bottom up solution,' Anand Mahindra said. It isn't the jugaad of cobbling together random parts to get by but a virtuous bypass. It's 'disintermediation' where 'you take away the intermediary. That's an elegant solution, in chess you call it a finesse,' he explained.

He gives the example of schools, where the application process is often corrupt and based on large upfront payments or the intervention of influential friends.

'When you remove intermediaries it prevents people looking for shortcuts. If you didn't have intermediaries, for example, in the schools, [if] the entire application was transparent and on the web, that is disintermediation, that would not be a bypass or jugaad, that would mean you are removing all those people who were making you take shortcuts,' he explained.

He believes it is the answer to those who say India suffers poverty, bad governance and poor infrastructure because it is so vast and the scale of its problems too daunting.

He once wrote an article in response to those who said tiny, smart and successful Singapore offered no solutions to the problems of a vast country like India.

'If we're too large to solve this problem, why don't we break ourselves up into smaller units? Why are we arguing about states being too large, let's become a hundred Singapores…disaggregate it and solve it rather than die hearing we're too large and can't solve it,' he said.

'You break up the problems. I'm not going back to Gandhi's "small is beautiful" because that had some romantic elements in it but today technology has answers,' he added.

Kaushik Basu, a former chief economist of the World Bank and chief economic adviser to the Government of India from 2009 to 2012, believes corruption—the incentive for many bad jugaad 'solutions'—could also be broken down into a more manageable problem that could be worked around. Instead of dealing with the problem head on—by establishing an anti-corruption force with draconian powers, like Hong Kong's Independent Commission

Against Corruption, for example—half of those involved could simply be decriminalized by legalizing the payment of bribes.

Much of the corruption India suffers is in the form of 'harassment bribes', demands by officials for kickbacks as the price of carrying out the ordinary duties they are paid to do.

'Suppose an income tax refund is held back from a taxpayer till he pays some cash to the officer. Suppose government allots subsidized land to a person but when the person goes to get her paperwork done and receive documents for this land, she is asked to pay a hefty bribe... Harassment bribery is widespread in India and it plays a large role in breeding inefficiency and has a corrosive effect on civil society,' he explained in an official paper.

Under current law the corrupt official and his victim have a mutual interest in covering up this extortion because once the payer has handed over the cash they are both guilty of the same crime.

By decriminalizing the victim 'the bribe giver and the bribe taker will be at divergence. The bribe giver will be willing to cooperate in getting the bribe taker caught. Knowing that this will happen, the bribe taker will be deterred from taking a bribe,' he explained.

Sam Pitroda looks every bit the telecom pioneer he is—a white shock of long Einstein hair, a guru goatee beard and a general air of creative mischief. Together with Nandan Nilekani, one of the founders of the Indian IT giant Infosys, he laid the foundations for what could be the greatest bypass in the history of independent India—one that could render Kashik Basu's proposal unnecessary.

After his appointment by previous prime minister Dr Manmohan Singh as an adviser on public information and innovation, Pitroda began connecting India's universities via 1,500 nodes with 40 gigabit cables. Then he started work on an optical fibre network to connect almost all of India's 265,000 village panchayats to broadband Internet.

Nandan Nilekani was given one of the world's most ambitious tasks in 2009 when the previous government asked him to create a digital database to record and store the identification details of every Indian.

Their tasks were complementary. With universal access to fast Internet services and an official digital record of their identity, every Indian would be able to open a bank account and have their benefits paid directly into it without dealing with an official who might demand a bribe for doing his job or not causing an unnecessary delay. They could simply bypass corrupt officialdom.

. It could revolutionize the way children learn and their families access healthcare. The teachers whose absenteeism hinders their learning could be bypassed and lessons taken online instead through study applications and video tutorials. Their parents may, one day, be able to access their own medical records and book hospital appointments. The computerization of police and court records could enable judges to clear the backlog of twenty-eight million pending cases in five to ten years instead of an estimated three centuries, Sam Pitroda explained: circumvention is India's best hope of progress and development.

'Most of my work in India has been basically geared towards creating a bypass around the system. The system is clogged everywhere!' he said. 'Existing systems just don't work. It's a sad commentary. Try to do as many bypasses or otherwise fix what you can. There's no sense in complaining about what it is. We all know the problems—this doesn't work, the roads are not good, no one follows traffic rules. There is corruption. You don't need talent to identify a problem or find a solution. You need talent to get it done against all the odds and in the existing system…if you wait for everything to be fixed, it will never happen.'

His solution is to create enough bypasses for them to become the new system.

Can India's cities, the encroachment of public land, the fatal driving on the roads, unsafe buildings, pollution of rivers and corrupt policing simply be bypassed?

Can India as it exists be worked around to create India as its visionaries imagine it? Are there good jugaad solutions for India's bad jugaad mess?

Sam Pitroda's ally Nandan Nilekani doesn't think so. He believes jugaad innovations and workarounds can be inspiring and heroic—they symbolize the irrepressible optimism of ordinary Indians in the face of systems which don't meet basic needs.

But they cannot be an alternative to developing the essential infrastructure and functioning systems the country needs if its people are to prosper.

'[If] you want a national system of roads, you have to build it properly, you can't do it jugaad-style. If you need 24/7 power, you need to do it properly,' he said.

His fear is that India becomes too enamoured with the idea of jugaad fixes and that the propensity of Indians to find their own individual solutions dissipates public pressure for better systems and basic infrastructure.

'It's a safety valve for the systemic reforms that you need…when people are able to find jugaad workarounds then the collective pressure of society to find a systemic solution to that problem diminishes,' he explained. India's rich have embraced their own individual solutions—private water purification, generators for guaranteed power, flights to avoid the trains—and seceded from India as it is experienced by the majority. 'That acts as a safety wall which militates against the fundamental reform that you need. If I fix my problem, I'm not bothered, no?' he said.

He believes the best answer is for India to build a sound base of physical and digital infrastructure—water and power supply, roads, sanitation, information technology, good schools and healthcare and online government services—and for people to be given free rein to make their own jugaad improvements and innovations on top.

'The fact that people have this innovative, entrepreneurial ability to come up with new solutions and deft ideas, that's great news, that's bottom-up innovation, but if you can give them a platform on which they can do it, if you can create something where everyone plays on one playing field, then you get the best of both worlds, you get the scale of a platform and the individual entrepreneurship of people. That's where we miss out. The fact is that we need platforms. If we can marry a platform to jugaad then we get the best of both worlds. That's the missing piece,' he explained.

How can that puzzle be completed? How can India create a culture in which sound systems can be built upon with inspiration and creativity rather than circumvented and sabotaged? How can it elevate good jugaad and purge the bad?

That battle will have to be waged in hearts and minds among a people long accustomed to working around problems and institutions to meet their needs. For many of them jugaad is not only a hard-won battle honour but a lifelong friend.

The first salvo may already have been fired. On 8 November 2016, the Indian prime minister announced the overnight scrapping of ₹500 and ₹1,000 currency notes as part of a crackdown on thousands of crores of rupees' worth of undeclared 'black money' and the widescale corruption and jugaad politics associated with it.

The move plunged India into panic and chaos. It was announced at the height of the country's wedding season in which lavish celebrations are paid in cash. Long queues formed outside banks and cash machines and many suffered considerable losses—most property transactions in India are part-paid for in undeclared cash and many people hoarded 'black money' because normal living required it.

Now, suddenly, they had to declare it or lose it. The government argued the move would, overnight, promote a more transparent economy, cashless card payments and bank transfers, and reduce scope for corruption.

While it has been fiercely criticized by opponents, it is too early to judge whether his dramatic and controversial initiative will eventually be a success. The symbolism, however, was unmistakable—India must embrace transparency and move away from the shady fixes and compromises of its Black Economy. Less noticed, but unmistakeable was another message celebrating the winning combination of Indian science, jugaad innovation and demanding standards of excellence.

On the same day, the government released the new ₹2,000 note with its statement of intent and vision for India's future on one side: a picture of the *Mangalyaan* in orbit around Mars.

One source of bad jugaad was put on notice as a winning combination of good jugaad innovation and Indian rocket science was immortalized on crisp new magenta banknotes.

In his speech to mark *Mangalyaan's* conquest of Mars, Modi set out its significance for the country's future and the new constellation of possibilities it opened for what Indians could achieve.

'We Indians are a proud people. Despite our many limitations, we aspire for the best. The success of our space programme is a shining example of what we are capable of as a nation. Our space programme has been an example of achievement, which inspires the rest of us to strive for excellence ourselves,' he said.

Its success had shown that frugal innovation need not mean cheap shoddy and that jugaad creativity and rocket science are not mutually exclusive. Indians could reject cut-price standards and demand excellence. They could refuse to be 70 per cent satisficers and become optimizers for glory.

The jugaad yatra marches on. Which way will it turn?

They could follow Modi's *Mangalyaan* map to a constellation of good jugaad innovation and Indian scientific excellence. They might just take the bypass instead.

The answer is in their pocket.

ACKNOWLEDGEMENTS

My jugaad yatra began just over halfway through our ten years in Delhi. I never imagined it would take so long or need so much support to complete it. So heartfelt thanks are due to all those who suffered as sounding boards and gave sage advice and encouragement when it was most needed: Pamela Timms, our family's best writer, who walked every mile of it with me; to Vir Sanghvi, Nilanjana Roy, Sir Mark Tully, Francis Elliott and Schona Jolly who kindly read the manuscript and shared their thoughts; and to all our Delhi friends, especially James Tapper and Marcus Winsley, whose enduring interest nudged me on. Special thanks are due to Jalees Andrabi who gently and patiently guided me throughout my time reporting on India, and to Tripta Narang who helped with research.

I also want to thank the many interviewees who gave their time generously even though their comments do not feature prominently in this edition, in particular to Professor Romila Thapar and Amar Singh. Their thoughts and comments helped shape the book.

Sincere thanks too to my publisher David Davidar and Aienla Ozukum at Aleph, Amardeep Banerjee, and my agent Marysia Juszczakiewicz at Peony Literary Agency for their patience.

NOTES AND REFERENCES

PROLOGUE: A JUGAAD YATRA

ix **Jugaad:** There are many definitions—one of the points of the book—but not a single, accepted one and this includes those from *Brihat Hindi Kosh*, and R. S. McGregor's *Oxford Hindi-English Dictionary*. Neither of these nor the new *Oxford English Dictionary* definition captures how the word is used in India.

ix **The seventh-largest economy in the world:** 'Gross domestic product 2016', *World Bank*, <http://databank.worldbank.org/data/download/GDP.pdf> [accessed 3 March 2018].

ix **projected to be the fifth largest:** H. S. Rao, 'India to become the fifth largest economy in 2018: CEBR report', *The Quint*, 30 December 2017 <https://www.thequint.com/news/india/indian-economy-to-be-5th-largest-in-2018-world-economic-league-table> [accessed 3 March 2018].

x **The secret of India's Mars Orbiter Mission:** Karine Schomer, 'Getting to Mars through "jugaad"', *The Hindu*, 8 October 2014 <http://www.thehindu.com/opinion/op-ed/Getting-to-Mars-through-%E2%80%98jugaad%E2%80%99/article11061060.ece> [accessed 3 March 2018].

x **This original jugaad was made possible:** It was first mentioned to me in an interview with Saurabh Srivastava, a member of the National Innovation Council.

xii **They'd cut corners, made do with recycled parts:** Krittivas Mukherjee, 'From lighter rocket to slingshot, Isro innovates its way to Mars', *Hindustan Times*, 24 September 2014 <https://

www.hindustantimes.com/india/from-lighter-rocket-to-slingshot-isro-innovates-its-way-to-mars/story-QDzE5Meiy0KrfGC0RfevrI. html> [accessed 3 March 2018].

xii **Indian approach of getting the maximum:** Schomer, 'Getting to Mars through "jugaad"'.

xiv **every Indian' into a 'master of jugaad':** Kamal Nath, *India's Century: The Age of Entrepreneurship in the World's Biggest Democracy,* New York: McGraw-Hill Professional, 2007.

xv **A culture of "jugaad", or creative improvisation:** Kirtsen Bound and Ian Thorton, *Our Frugal Future: Lessons from India's Innovation System,* Nesta, July 2012 <https://www.nesta.org.uk/sites/default/files/our_frugal_future.pdf> [accessed 3 March 2018].

xv **First, it is frugal:** Ibid., quoted in *Jugaad Innovation: Think Frugal, Be Flexible, Generate Breakthrough Growth.*

xv **practised by almost all Indians:** Navi Radjou, Jaideep Prabhu and Simone Ahuja, J*ugaad Innovation: Think Frugal, Be Flexible, Generate Breakthrough Growth,* San Francisco: Wiley Books, 2012, p. 5.

xvi **One US diplomat reported:** '162458: Cash-for-votes ahead of confidence motion', *The Hindu,* 17 March 2011 <http://www.thehindu.com/news/the-india-cables/the-cables/162458-Cash-for-votes-ahead-of-confidence-motion/article14962596.ece> [accessed 3 March 2018].

xvi **India's 'biggest jugaad':** My interview with Amar Singh.

xvii **some of the mismanagement:** Sujay Mehdudia, 'CAG pins 700-page medal of shame on Delhi, Centre', *The Hindu,* 5 August 2011 <http://www.thehindu.com/news/national/cag-pins-700page-medal-of-shame-on-delhi-centre/article2328222.ece> [accessed 3 March 2018].

xviii **Today's India is chaotic:** My interview with Bharatbala.

xx **Through the questions that emerge:** My interview with Amish Tripathi.

xxi **decide how best to order their lives:** My interview with Gurcharan Das.

xxii Anatomy and surgery became 'lost sciences': Praphulla Chandra Ray, *A History of Hindu Chemistry*, London: Williams and Norgate, 1902, pp. 106-107.

xxii In her essay on jugaad thinking: Schomer, 'Getting to Mars through "jugaad"'.

xxii smashed their thumbs, broke their looms: 'Shashi Tharoor's full speech asking UK to pay India for 200 years of its colonial rule', *News18*, 24 July 2015 <https://www.news18.com/news/india/read-shashi-tharoors-full-speech-asking-uk-to-pay-india-for-200-years-of-its-colonial-rule-1024821.html> [accessed 4 March 2018].

CHAPTER 1: SNOWBREEZE

2 'assembled from scratch at home': Kunal Diwan, 'Beating the heat with a home-made AC', *The Hindu*, 26 February 2008 <http://www.thehindu.com/todays-paper/tp-national/tp-newdelhi/Beating-the-heat-with-a-home-made-AC/article15173700.ece> [accessed 4 March 2018].

2 to pay the bribes needed: My interview with M. B. Lal. Mr Lal suggests it was for bribes to speed local support for the canal to be built but also that the East India Company officer may have been making money too.

6 world's largest two-wheeler bicycle manufacturer: Naveen Soni, 'Hero MotoCorp scores over 175 touch points in Haryana, more than 6,500 across India', *Times of India*, 25 February 2018 <https://timesofindia.indiatimes.com/auto/bikes/hero-motocorp-scores-over-175-touch-points-in-haryana-more-than-6500-across-india/articleshow/63066129.cms> [accessed 19 March 2018].

8 India is home to one-third: 'India has highest number of people living below poverty line: World Bank', *Business Today*, 3 October 2016 <https://www.businesstoday.in/current/economy-politics/india-has-highest-number-of-people-living-below-poverty-line-world-bank/story/238085.html> [accessed 4 March 2018].

CHAPTER 2: SWADESHI R & D

12 **one district administration is even considering:** Ritesh Mishra, 'MP:Radium tape for cows to reduce accidents', *Hindustan Times*, 15 July 2016 <https://www.hindustantimes. com/indore/mp-radium-tape-for-cows-to-reduce-accidents/story-D0WBoHI80XLysTQIAohZyO.html> [accessed 4 March 2018].

13 **'He's slowly made his way through':** My interview with Professor Anil Gupta.

14 **We used a tin box:** My interview with Dharamveer Kamboj.

20 **I realized that picking is not difficult:** My interview with Nathubhai Vadha.

21 **why only 12 per cent of India's women:** Vibeke Venema, 'The Indian sanitary pad revolutionary', *BBC*, 4 March 2014 < http://www.bbc.com/news/magazine-26260978> [accessed 8 March 2018].

21 **teenage girls miss fifty days of school every year:** Kounteya Sinha, '70% can't afford sanitary napkins, reveals study', *Times of India*, 23 January 2011 <https://timesofindia.indiatimes.com/india/70-cant-afford-sanitary-napkins-reveals-study/articleshow/7344998. cms> [accessed 8 March 2014].

22 **artist and sculptor Ram Chandra Sharma:** While both Sharma and Dr P. K. Sethi are credited with the invention of the Jaipur Foot, my focus here is on the innovation part of it, which was Sharma's rather than that of Dr Sethi's. Dr Sethi was the orthopaedic surgeon who gave expert assistance.

23 **restricts us to the use and service:** M. K. Gandhi, 'Definition of swadeshi', 1916 < http://www.mkgandhi.org/articles/swadeshi1. htm> [accessed 8 March 2018]

24 **'inherently violent':** Fritz Schumacher, *Small Is Beautiful: A Study of Economics As If People Mattered*, London: Blond & Briggs Ltd., 1973, p. 126.

CHAPTER 3: CROREPATIS: THE JUGAAD GUIDE TO MAKING BILLIONS

34 I don't want my forces being stretched: Arjun Sen and Aloke Tikku, 'IPL not keen to toe Home Minister's line', *Hindustan Times*, 3 March 2009 <https://www.hindustantimes. com/cricket/ipl-not-keen-to-toe-home-minister-s-line/story-4njS0BbnojNVXvGTR9ZcMI.html> [accessed 11 March 2018].

34 head of the Disney entertainment: He's referring to Lalit Modi hiring Etienne de Villiers who had been a senior Disney executive.

44 a claim by the leader: 'Team Anna sees conspiracy in northern power grid collapse', *Economic Times*, 30 July 2012 <https://economictimes.indiatimes.com/news/politics-and-nation/team-anna-sees-conspiracy-in-northern-power-grid-collapse/articleshow/15276302.cms?intenttarget=no> [accessed 11 March 2018].

44 one-third of those living in rural areas: Rama Lakshmi and Simon Denyer, 'Lack of power symbolizes India's inequalities', 6 August 2012 <https://www.washingtonpost.com/world/asia_pacific/lack-of-power-symbolizes-indias-inequalities/2012/08/06/ecdbef64-df20-11e1-a19c-fcfa365396c8_story.html?utm_term=.6aa6e61d4be1> [accessed 11 March 2018]. Today, the percentage without electricity is 25 per cent.

CHAPTER 4: 'FOR MOST INDIANS 70 PER CENT IS GOOD ENOUGH'

50 A survey in villages near Hubli: *Saathi Report–Jayashree Industries* commissioned by Bhoruka Charitable Trust, 2012. The report is based on interviews with women in the Hubli-Dharwad area.

53 world's cheapest Metro system: 'News in numbers: Delhi Metro is the cheapest in the world', *Livemint*, 12 September 2016. <http://www.livemint.com/Politics/megFsFe64jgERms2AzknQN/News-in-numbers--Delhi-Metro-is-the-cheapest-in-the-world.html> [accessed 12 March 2018].

53 **three years ahead of schedule:** 'Delhi Metro: Setting an example in India', *Global Mass Transit,* 1 May 2010 <https://www.globalmasstransit.net/archive.php?id=2946> [accessed 12 March 2018].

53 **He donated his salary to charity:** Mamuni Das, 'Metroman, may your tribe increase', *Hindu BusinessLine* 2016 <https://www.thehindubusinessline.com/opinion/metroman-may-your-tribe-increase/article8349044.ece> [accessed 12 March 2018].

54 **'damp squib':** '$10-laptop proves to be a damp squib', *Times of India,* 4 February 2009 <https://timesofindia.indiatimes.com/city/hyderabad/10-laptop-proves-to-be-a-damp-squib/articleshow/4072417.cms> [accessed 12 March 2018].

54 **one in three of the tech giant:** Shilpa Phadnis and Sujit John, 'One in every 3 Apple engineers is Indian', *Times of India,* 28 July 2014 <https://www.gadgetsnow.com/tech-news/One-in-every-3-Apple-engineers-is-Indian/articleshow/39131973.cms> [accessed 12 March 2018].

55 **Just over half of secondary age children:** 'Statistics', *UNICEF,* 2013 <https://www.unicef.org/infobycountry/india_statistics.html> [accessed 12 March 2018].

59 **as a 'stopping mechanism':** Gerd Gigerenzer and Reinhard Selten. ed., *Bounded Reality,* 2001, p. 42. <http://www.jayhanson.us/_Biology/BoundedRationality_TheAdaptiveToolbox.pdf> [accessed 12 March 2018].

59 **'backwoods mechanic and used-parts dealer':** Ibid., p. 43.

60 **fastest growing mobile phone market:** Saritha Rai, 'World's fastest-growing smartphone market could become a manufacturing hub', *Bloomberg,* 21 November 2006 <https://www.bloomberg.com/news/articles/2016-11-21/india-seeks-manufacturing-jobs-as-smartphone-market-takes-off> [accessed 12 March 2018].

60 **despite being home to 400 million:** 'The state of the poor: where are the poor and where are they poorest?' *World Bank* <http://www.worldbank.org/content/dam/Worldbank/document/State_of_the_poor_paper_April17.pdf> [accessed 12 March 2018].

61 develop a credible low-cost device had failed: My interview with Suneet Singh Tuli.

CHAPTER 5: BAD JUGAAD

70 with the front of a Harley: Harley Davidson bikes mass produced during World War II were modified into 'jugaad trikes' used to ply as public transport on the streets of Delhi.

71 a Six Sigma rating of 99.9999: Beena Parmar, 'Mumbai's dabbawalas up delivery charges by Rs. 100', *Hindu BusinessLine*, 2 July 2014 <https://www.thehindubusinessline.com/news/mumbais-dabbawalas-up-delivery-charges-by-100/article20810873.ece> [accessed 13 March 2018].

74 India's biggest producer of generic drugs: It is no longer the biggest, but was previously.

74 In May 2013, Ranbaxy Usa, Inc. pleaded guilty: 'Ranbaxy pleads guilty, to pay $500 mln in settlement', *Reuters*, 13 May 2013 <https://in.reuters.com/article/ranbaxy-settlement-felony-usa/ranbaxy-pleads-guilty-to-pay-500-mln-in-settlement-idINDEE94C0DA20130513> [accessed 14 March 2018].

74 His evidence to the United States Food and Drugs Administration: My interview with Dinesh Thakur.

74 the MHRA recalled sixteen Wockhardt medicines: pharmaceutical-journal.com, 'Manufacturing site deficiencies prompt Wockhardt medicines recall', *Pharmaceutical Journal*, 18 October 2013 <https://www.pharmaceutical-journal.com/news-and-analysis/manufacturing-site-deficiencies-prompt-wockhardt-medicines-recall/11128870.article> [accessed 14 March 2018].

75 why we have come to accept poor governance: Dinesh Thakur, 'The Indian way? No way', *The Hindu*, 12 June 2013 <http://www.thehindu.com/opinion/op-ed/the-indian-way-no-way/article4804513.ece> [accessed 14 March 2018].

75 There are unacceptable problems with drugs: 'Statements for Hill briefing on FDA, India and substandard drugs', *Searching for Safety*, 2014 <http://www.searchingforsafety.net/

uploads/2/6/2/1/26218021/speakers_statements_hill_event.pdf>
[accessed 14 March 2014].

76 **The effects of these impurities could be toxic:** My interview
    with Dr R. Preston Mason.

76 **cutting corners to boost:** My interview with Roger Bate.

77 **Victorian Royal Infirmaries:** Decaying hospitals built in the
    Georgian and Victorian periods, some of them more than 200 years
    old.

78 **six feet tall with typical TDH:** 'Anuradha's Story', *People for
    Better Treatment* <https://pbtindia.wordpress.com/anuradhas-story/>
    [accessed 14 March 2018].

79 **'culpable of civil liabilities':** Vidya Krishnan, 'Medical
    negligence: Will the Anuradha Saha case set a precedent?',
    Livemint, 6 November 2013 <http://www.livemint.com/Politics/
    rYITtOKCr3IO0iexKbvc6K/Medical-negligence-Will-Anuradha-
    Saha-case-set-precedent.html> [accessed 14 March 2018].

79 **669 of whom were suspended or struck off:** Sarah Knapton,
    'Half of foreign doctors are below British standards', *The Telegraph*, 18
    April 2014. <https://www.telegraph.co.uk/news/nhs/10773857/
    Half-of-foreign-doctors-are-below-British-standards.html>
    [accessed 14 March 2018].

79 **There is a perception that doctors:** My interview with Dr
    Kunal Saha.

79 **an explanation for unnecessary surgeries:** 'Satyamev Jayate
    - Does Healthcare Need Healing? - 27th May 2012' *YouTube*, 26
    May 2012 <https://www.youtube.com/watch?v=1Lg0kUtS8ic>
    [accessed 16 March 2018].

80 **I can't have children:** Ibid.

80 **Doctors are too busy to study:** My interview with Dr Kunal
    Saha.

80 **a number of doctors lowering costs:** Shobita Dhar, 'Surgeons
    do jugaad in the operation theatre', *Times of India*, 17 February 2014
    <https://timesofindia.indiatimes.com/india/Surgeons-do-jugaad-
    in-the-operation-theatre/articleshow/30491175.cms> [accessed 16

March 2018].

81 **Investigations and procedures are abused:** David Berger, 'Corruption ruins the doctor-patient relationship in India', *The BMJ*, 8 May 2014 < http://www.bmj.com/content/348/bmj. g3169> [accessed 16 March 2018].

82 **'unsafe and unfit for human habitation':** Andrew Buncombe and Robin Scott-Elliot, 'A bridge too far? Race to keep Commonwealth Games on track', *The Independent*, 21 September 2010 <https://www. independent.co.uk/sport/general/athletics/a-bridge-too-far-race-to-keep-commonwealth-games-on-track-2085854.html> [accessed 16 March 2018].

82 **There have been dogs roaming:** Amlan Chakraborty, 'India battles to save scandal-hit Commonwealth Games', *Reuters*, 22 September 2010 <https://www.reuters.com/article/us-games/india-battles-to-save-scandal-hit-commonwealth-games-idUSTRE68K2XX20100922> [accessed 16 March 2018].

82 **Indian officials had evicted him:** My interview with Mike Hooper.

82 **With only a year to run:** Dean Nelson, 'Delhi Commonwealth Games "at grave risk of collapse"', *The Telegraph*, 15 September 2009 <https://www.telegraph.co.uk/news/worldnews/asia/india/6190118/Delhi-Commonwealth-Games-at-grave-risk-of-collapse.html?mobile=basic> [accessed 16 March 2018].

83 **In the village he has no chance:** Dean Nelson and Jacquelin Magnay, 'Commonwealth Games 2010: injured labourer abandoned', *The Independent*, 6 October 2010 <https://www. telegraph.co.uk/sport/othersports/commonwealthgames/8046587/Commonwealth-Games-2010-injured-labourer-abandoned.html> [accessed 16 March 2018].

84 **All the warning signs were there:** 'Commonwealth Games' chief executive rejects blame for Delhi crisis', *The Guardian*, 26 September 2010. <https://www.theguardian.com/sport/2010/sep/26/commonwealth-games-blame-delhi-crisis> [accessed 16 March 2018].

84 **'The processing of certain sensitive contracts:** 'Audit Report in XIXth Commonwealth Games 2010', *Comptroller and Auditor General of India*, 2011-12, p. 563 <http://www.cag.gov.in/sites/default/files/audit_report_files/Union_Performance_Civil_XIXth_Commonwealth_Games_6_2011.pdf> [accessed 16 March 2018].

84 **it was left to the eleventh hour:** My interview with Vinod Rai.

86 **When the world goes for gold:** Vinod Rai, 'Pursuit of excellence—role of governance', Comptroller and Auditor General, speech to IIMPM, Bhubaneswar, 20 January 2013.

88 **A reason for our lack of excellence:** Ibid.

CHAPTER 6: A RIVER RUNS THROUGH IT

91 **almost 600 million of them:** bbc.com, 'India census: Half of homes have phones but no toilets', *BBC*, 14 March 2012 <http://www.bbc.com/news/world-asia-india-17362837> [accessed 16 March 2018].

91 **deaths of 750,000 children:** Emily Carter, Jennifer Bryce, Jamie Perin and Holly Newby, 'Harmful practices in the management of childhood diarrhea in low- and middle-income countries: a systematic review', *NCBI*, 18 August 2015 <https://www.ncbi.nlm.nih.gov/pmc/articles/PMC4538749/> [accessed 16 March 2018].

91 **'India is drowning in its own excreta':** *Excreta Matters, How Urban India is Soaking Up Water, Polluting Rivers, and Drowning In Its Own Excreta*, Centre for Science and Environment, 2012, preface by Sunita Narain.

91 **More Indians own mobile phones:** 'India census: Half of homes have phones but no toilets', *BBC*, 14 March, 2012 < http://www.bbc.com/news/world-asia-india-17362837> [accessed 30 April 2018].

95 **'It's with small chores that big goals:** Dean Nelson, 'Narendra Modi vows to clean up pollution in India', *The Telegraph*, 26 May 2014 <https://www.telegraph.co.uk/news/worldnews/asia/india/10855190/Narendra-Modi-vows-to-clean-up-pollution-in-India.html> [accessed 16 March 2018].

97 **Near the bridges the feculence rolled:** M. Faraday, 'Observations

on the filth of the Thames, contained in a letter addressed to the Editor of "The Times" Newspaper, by Professor Faraday', 7 July 1855 <http://www.chemteam.info/Chem-History/Faraday-Letter.html> [accessed 16 March 2018].

98 **urban India is soaking up water:** *Excreta Matters*, p. XX, and also my interview with Sunita Narain.

98 **India's main Class One and Class Two cities:** *Excreta Matters*, Vol 2, p. 97.

98 **In 2011, the city generated:** Ibid., p. 79.

98 **half the population of Delhi:** Dhananjay Mahapatra, 'Half of Delhi's population lives in slums', *Times of India*, 4 October 2012 <https://timesofindia.indiatimes.com/city/delhi/Half-of-Delhis-population-lives-in-slums/articleshow/16664224.cms> [accessed 16 March 2018].

98 **A 2009 survey of slums:** *Excreta Matters*, Vol. 1, p. 91.

98 **they generate just 5 per cent of waste:** Ibid., p. 90.

99 **enjoy 462 litres per capita per day:** Ibid, Vol. 2, p. 85.

100 **estimated to generate Rs. 2,000 crore per year:** 'A look into the dark and dangerous world of illegal sand mining', *India Today*, 4 August 2013 <https://www.indiatoday.in/india/north/story/illegal-sand-mining-corruption-and-turf-wars-172695-2013-08-04> [accessed 17 March 2018].

100 **have her suspended within forty-one minutes:** 'SP leader brags he got Nagpal suspended in 41 minutes', *The Hindu*, 2 August 2013 <http://www.thehindu.com/news/national/sp-leader-brags-he-got-nagpal-suspended-in-41-minutes/article4981198.ece> [accessed 17 March 2018].

101 **'Everyone has the right on nature's bounty:** Dean Nelson, '"Loot as much as you can of nature" says Indian minister', *The Telegraph*, 1 August 2013 <https://www.telegraph.co.uk/news/worldnews/asia/india/10215936/Loot-as-much-as-you-can-of-nature-says-Indian-minister.html> [accessed 17 March 2018].

101 **'loud and clear' message from the state government:** 'IAS Durga Shakti Nagpal's suspension an example of mafia raj: Mayawati',

Times of India, 1 August 2013 <https://timesofindia.indiatimes.com/india/ias-durga-shakti-nagpals-suspension-an-example-of-mafia-raj-mayawati/articleshow/21521851.cms> [accessed 17 March 2018].

101 **dig out the river's bed:** Akash Vashishtha, 'Sand mafia flourishes: A year after the Durga Nagpal episode, mining on Yamuna bed continues', 4 May 2014, *Daily Mail*, 4 May 2014 <http://www.dailymail.co.uk/indiahome/indianews/article-2619707/Sand-mafia-flourishes-A-year-Durga-Nagpal-episode-mining-Yamuna-bed-flourishes.html> [accessed 17 March 2018].

101 **inspection by the Environmental Pollution (Control and Prevention) Authority:** *Excreta Matters*, vol. 2, p. 96.

101 **'But I see it is there in a major way:** My interview with Himanshu Thakkar.

103 **the world's biggest 'open air toilet':** 'Indian rail is world's largest "open toilet"': Jairam Ramesh', *NDTV*, 27 July 2012 <https://www.ndtv.com/india-news/indian-rail-is-worlds-largest-open-toilet-jairam-ramesh-494434> [accessed 17 March 2018].

103 **inefficiency or corruption by bypassing rules:** My interview with Jairam Ramesh.

CHAPTER 7: THE GRAND TRUNK ROAD TO NOWHERE

108 **the world's most dangerous roads:** Suparna Dutt D'Cunha, 'Infrastructure: Is India driven to improve?' *Gulf News*, 18 August 2016 <http://gulfnews.com/gn-focus/country-guides/reports/india/infrastructure-is-india-driven-to-improve-1.1877660> [accessed 17 March 2018].

109 **the leading Indian car manufacturer:** Ronak Shah, 'Top 10 car manufacturers in India: Know car makers market share in 2017', *Financial Express*, 11 January 2018 <http://www.financialexpress.com/auto/car-news/top-10-car-manufacturers-in-india-know-car-makers-market-share-in-2017/1011187/> [accessed 17 March 2018].

109 **They say we'll train you:** My interview with Kiran Kapila.

116 **meeting for all road safety stakeholders:** Ragini Verma,

'Nitin Gadkari calls meeting on road safety standards on Thursday', *Livemint*, 4 June 2014 <http://www.livemint.com/Politics/ Hc96mCQmIIZpXLNvtDap4O/Nitin-Gadkari-calls-meeting-on-road-safety-standards-on-Thur.html> [accessed 17 March 2018].

116 **he was baffled at the move:** Rumu Banerjee, 'Not regulating e-rickshaws a bad idea: Experts', *Times of India*, 18 June 2014 <https://timesofindia.indiatimes.com/city/delhi/Not-regulating-e-rickshaws-a-bad-idea-Experts/articleshow/36728013.cms> [accessed 17 March 2018].

CHAPTER 8: URBAN JUGAAD: INDIA'S CITIES IN CRISIS

118 **drop all their rubbish on the road outside:** Damini Nath, 'Workers litter for Minister to clean up', *The Hindu,* 26 Septmber 2014 <http://www.thehindu.com/news/cities/Delhi/workers-litter-for-minister-to-clean-up/article6448326.ece> [accessed on 17 March 2018].

119 **officials outsourced their planned sweep:** Ayaskant Das, 'CHILD LABOUR - Kids used in Hindon cleanup, finds probe', *Times of India,* 15 October 2014 <http://epaperbeta.timesofindia.com/ Article.aspx?eid=31808&articlexml=CHILD-LABOUR-Kids-used-in-Hindon-cleanup-finds-15102014007019> [accessed 17 March 2018].

119 **dirty, dangerous, unsightly, poor:** Ratish Nanda, 'The problem', *India Seminar* <http://www.india-seminar.com/2014/657/657_ problem.htm> [accessed 17 March 2018].

119 **ten of the world's twenty most polluted cities:** Nick Van Mead, 'Pant by numbers: the cities with the most dangerous air – listed', *The Guardian,* 13 February 2017 <https://www.theguardian.com/ cities/datablog/2017/feb/13/most-polluted-cities-world-listed-region> [accessed 17 March 2018].

120 **Only 2,100 of the 5,000 tonnes of rubbish:** Naveen B. P. and Sivapullaiah P. V., 'Solid waste management in Bengaluru-current scenario and future challenges', *Innovative Energy and Research*, 25 August 2016 <https://www.omicsonline.org/open-

access/solid-waste-management-in-bengalurucurrent-scenario-and-futurechallenges-.php?aid=78824> [accessed 17 March 2018].

121 **Its then chief minister had believed:** Anisha Bhatia, 'After 17 years, garbage bins make a comeback in Bengaluru to support government's two-bin policy', *NDTV*, 22 June 2017 <http://swachhindia.ndtv.com/17-years-garbage-bins-make-comeback-bengaluru-support-governments-two-bin-policy-9036/> [accessed 17 March 2018].

121 **This is a great environment for wildlife:** Anamik Nagrik, 'INTRO', *The Ugly Indian* <http://theuglyindian.com/books/> [accessed 17 March 2018].

122 **'tragedy of the commons':** The term is used to describe the damage done by individuals when there is no personal ownership or responsibility. For example, when people start walking across a public lawn as a short cut, damaging the grass, others follow because it becomes well-trodden. It is ruined by lack of responsibility, ownership and self-interest.

123 **sick of waiting for someone else:** Anamik Nagrik, 'INTRO'.

123 **It's time we admitted that many:** Anamik Nagrik, 'The Ugly Indian: Is There Any Hope?', *The Ugly Indian* <http://www.theuglyindian.com/intro1.html> [accessed on 17 March 2018].

124 **'I know that in India throwing rubbish:** Arthur Martin and Tamara Cohen, 'Tory councillor "sorry" she blamed Indians for litter thrown out of the windows', *Daily Mail,* 11 June 2008 <http://www.dailymail.co.uk/news/article-1025615/Tory-councillor-sorry-blamed-Indians-litter-thrown-windows.html> [accessed on 17 March 2018].

125 **thick band of red—a sacred colour:** Anil Kumar said: 'Red is considered a sacred colour in south Indian temples. What we have done is when a wall is not looked after, we put in a band of red. If a place looks dirty, people will dirty it. If it looks like it deserves respect, it will get respect. When you do a rangoli it signifies sacred space.'

125 **then-existing no-bins policy:** In 2000, Karnataka's chief minister

S. M. Krishna banned public dustbins in an attempt to force people to keep their rubbish at home, separate it for collection, in the hope that the city could become a new Singapore.

127 **'world's largest beach clean-up project':** Medhavi Arora, 'From filthy to fabulous: Mumbai beach undergoes dramatic makeover', *CNN*, 22 May 2017 <https://edition.cnn.com/2017/05/22/asia/mumbai-beach-dramatic-makeover/index.html> [accessed on 17 March 2018].

127 **Eighty per cent of Delhi's houses:** '80 percent of Delhi's buildings illegal: MCD tells HC', *Rediff*, 18 January 2006 <http://www.rediff.com/news/2006/jan/18delhi1.htm> [accessed on 17 March 2018].

127 **illegal construction on either side:** 'Delhi: 10 dead after building collapse', *Hindustan Times*, 29 June 2014 <https://www.hindustantimes.com/delhi-news/delhi-10-dead-after-building-collapse/story-MppvWyfQpo5l22vU03nV0M.html> [accessed on 17 March 2018].

134 **ability to creatively "manage", to make do:** Kamal Nath: *India's Century*, p. 3.

134 **'suppressed Indian inventive gene':** Ibid., p. 4.

134 **Growth has preceded environment:** My interview with Kamal Nath.

138 **In India, what do we have?:** Dean Nelson, 'Indian tycoon plans a revolution', *The Times*, 8 October 2006 <https://www.thetimes.co.uk/article/indian-tycoon-plans-a-revolution-tmgw7wmjczt> [accessed 17 March 2018].

140 **alleged irregularities in land deals:** 'IAS officer Ashok Khemka transferred again', *Hindu BusinessLine*, 4 April 2013 <https://www.thehindubusinessline.com/news/ias-officer-ashok-khemka-transferred-again/article23088876.ece> [accessed 18 March 2018].

141 **after he submitted a report:** Sumedha Sharma, 'Two days after land-grab report, Kasni transferred', *Tribune India* 30 December 2014 <http://www.tribuneindia.com/news/haryana/two-days-after-land-grab-report-kasni-transferred/24095.html> [accessed 18 March 2018].

141 transferred seventy-one times: '71 Transfers in 34 Yrs: Curious Case of IAS Officer Pradeep Kasni', *The Quint,* 1 March 2018 <https://www.thequint.com/news/india/ias-pradeep-kasni-71-transfers-in-34-years> [accessed 18 March 2018].

141 I had already said yes: My interview with Pradeep Kasni.

142 the world's third wealthiest country: Lisa Marie Segarra, 'These are the richest countries in the world', *Fortune,* 17 November 2017 <http://fortune.com/2017/11/17/richest-country-in-the-world/> [accessed 18 March 2018].

143 Singapore was not dissimilar to Old Delhi: My interview with Liu Thai Ker.

CHAPTER 9: YATRA'S END: A T-POINT ON JUGAAD MARG

148 By 2024, India's population: 'India's population to surpass that of China around 2024: UN', *Times of India,* 21 June 2017 https://timesofindia.indiatimes.com/india/indias-population-to-surpass-that-of-chinas-around-2024-un/articleshow/59257045.cms [accessed 18 March 2018].

148 expected to reach 1.66 billion: Ibid.

148 We create the hardware: My interview with Sunita Narain.

149 To me that is the answer: My interview with Anand Mahindra.

151 Suppose an income tax refund: Kaushik Basu, 'Why, for a class of bribes, the act of giving a bribe should be treated as legal', March 2011 <http://www.kaushikbasu.org/Act_Giving_Bribe_Legal.pdf> [accessed 18 March 2018].

151 began connecting India's universities: 'Telecom revolution in India and the government's role in making it happen (or not)', *IEEE Communications Society,* 26 June 2012 <http://techblog.comsoc.org/2012/06/26/telecom-revolution-in-india-and-the-governments-role-in-making-it-happen-or-not/> [accessed 18 March 2018] and interview with me.

152 Most of my work in India: My interview with Sam Pitroda.

153 [If] you want a national system of roads: My interview with Nandan Nilekani.

155 We Indians are a proud people: 'Text of PM's address on the historic successful insertion of Mangalyaan into Martian orbit', *Times of India*, 24 September 2014 <https://timesofindia.indiatimes.com/india/Text-of-PMs-address-on-the-historic-successful-insertion-of-Mangalyaan-into-Martian-orbit/articleshow/43315741.cms> [accessed 18 March 2018].